WATER IN LANDSCAPE ARCHITECTURE

WATER IN LANDSCAPE ARCHITECTURE

ARCHITECTURE

DESIGN FUNCTIONS, PRINCIPLES, AND PROCEDURES

CRAIG S. CAMPBELL

VNR VAN NOSTRAND REINHOLD COMPANY
NEW YORK CINCINNATI TORONTO LONDON MELBOURNE

First published in paperback in 1982

Copyright © 1978 by Van Nostrand Reinhold Company Inc.

Library of Congress Catalog Card Number 77-24952

IBSN 0-442-21589-4

Printed in the United States of America

Designed by Loudan Enterprises

Drawings by Dorothy Shinn Nettle

Van Nostrand Reinhold Company Inc.
135 West 50th Street, New York, NY 10020

Van Nostrand Reinhold Publishing
1410 Birchmount Road, Scarborough, Ontario M1P 2E7

Van Nostrand Reinhold Australia Pty. Ltd.
480 Latrobe Street, Melbourne, Victoria 3000, Australia

Van Nostrand Reinhold Company Ltd.
Molly Millars Lane, Wokingham, Berkshire, England RG11 2PY

Cloth edition published 1978 by Van Nostrand Reinhold Company

16   15   14   13   12   11 10   9   8   7   6   5   4   3   2   1

CONTENTS

ACKNOWLEDGMENTS

Special thanks are due to the following individuals, who freely gave their time and expertise to discuss water features in design: Richard Chaix, Fountain Consultant, Oakland, California; Jack Erbe, President, Roman Fountains, Albuquerque, New Mexico; Byron McCulley, Lawrence Halprin & Associates, San Francisco, California.

My thanks also to the firms and agencies that provided photos, working drawings, or technical information on water features: William H. Behnke Associates, Cleveland, Ohio; Brown/Heldt Associates, San Francisco, California; Browning Day Pollak Associates, Carmel, Indiana; Andreas Bruun, Lyngby, Denmark; EDAW, Inc., Denver, Colorado; Flatow, Moore, Bryan & Associates, Albuquerque, New Mexico; Fong & LaRocca, San Francisco/ Newport Beach, California; Fort Worth Park and Recreation Department, Texas; M. Paul Friedberg & Associates, New York City; John E. Green Co., Inc., Highland Park, Michigan; Lawrence Halprin & Associates, San Francisco, California; Hydrel Corporation, Sun Valley, California; Johnson, Leffingwell & Associates, San Francisco, California; Kim Lighting, Inc., City of Industry, California; Morten Klint & Knud Lund-Sorensen, Copenhagen, Denmark; Derek Lovejoy & Partners, Manchester, England; Hans Luz & Partners, Stuttgart, Germany; Robert Marvin & Associates, Waterboro, South Carolina; Edward McCleod & Associates, Seattle, Washington; Minneapolis Department of Public Works; Mitchell & Associates, Portland, Oregon; Myrick, Newman, Dahlberg, Inc., Dallas, Texas; Kansas City Park & Recreation Department; Ben Notkin & Associates, Seattle, Washington; Noguchi Fountain & Plaza, Inc., Long Island City, New York; Ole Norgard, Copenhagen, Denmark; Theodore Osmundson & Associates, San Francisco, California; The Pea Group, Michigan City, Indiana; Michael Painter & Associates, San Francisco, California; PEM Fountain Company, Richmond Hill, Ontario, Canada; Royston, Hanamoto, Beck & Abey, Mill Valley, California; Sasaki Associates, Watertown, Massachusetts; Seattle Center Administration; Seattle Water Department; Saint Paul (Minnesota) Housing & Redevelopment Agency; Singer & Hodges, Oakland, California; Spink Corporation, Sacramento, California; John Sue Associates, Oakland, California; SWA Group, Sausalito, California; Prof. Bernhard Winkler, Munich, Germany.

The Dumbarton Oaks Garden Library in Washington, D.C. provided photos of engravings from Falda's *Le Fontane di Roma* (1675). The research for this book was aided in part by a grant from the National Endowment for the Arts, Washington, D.C.

INTRODUCTION

Water. It is difficult to imagine another element in the world that is so central and so vital both to basic life and to a diverse range of aesthetic and recreational pleasures, yet, in this era of specialization, it is almost impossible to find a book or study that accepts its infinite roles and qualities. The overwhelming majority of published volumes on water treat it strictly from the engineering viewpoint, dealing with dams, watersheds, and pollution control. In past ages the poet and the sculptor played as important a role as the engineer in giving form to the environment: for example, they were responsible for most of the early gardens in China and Japan, creating ideal images of water, rock and plant forms with methods incompatible with the western reliance on scaled drawings. In Renaissance Italy architects and engineers collaborated with sculptors in the creation of waterworks that utilized an incredible array of sophisticated devices, operating through the use of steam, differential pressure, pulleys, and hydrostatic principles that originated with the Greeks many centuries earlier.

I have tried in this volume to touch on many aspects of water but certainly not all. The designer of water features today should possess an understanding of the history of water in design as well as a grasp of the technical properties and limitations of water. With all the sophisticated advances in other areas of science and technology the fundamental principles of hydraulics have remained essentially the same for over a century. This text hopefully offers a useful resource to professional designers involved in water-feature design as well as to those interested in the subject but bewildered by the lack of good reference material.

1. WATER IN NATURE

The subject of water in nature is so encompassing that I can only touch briefly on it here. Depending upon climate, the quality of light, geology, soil, and a host of other factors, water can be reflective and moody, crystalline and sparkling, auditory and awesome. It is without question the supreme sculptor of our environment and a seductive attraction of most wilderness areas. Of the powerful fascination of the oceans enough has been written and painted.

As water flows from creek to stream and finally into a large river, it represents the link between mountain and ocean and more than any other element is responsible for the form and character of the landscape through which it passes. Although a stream or river may change its personality many times within its course, it provides a unifying element that identifies vast landscape or geographical regions (such as the Rio Grande Valley, the Mississippi Valley, the Grand Canyon, or the Columbia Basin).

Cascades and waterfalls seem to impart more of a sense of excitement and inspiration than calmer stretches of water, partly because the rocky setting of such features is wilder and more dramatic than broad, flat river valleys but also because of the visible discharge of energy that is produced in any such situation. It is interesting to note that the Japanese have many different classifications of waterfalls, depending upon the nature of the particular drop. In Chinese landscape painting waterfalls and pools are also a favored subject and are portrayed with a perfection that in my opinion has never been surpassed. A waterfall naturally creates its own immediate aesthetic "frame" and is therefore the center of the composition in which it is found. No two waterfalls are exactly alike: the infinite variety depends upon flow rate, height, channel-rock material, climate, sun angle, vegetation, and surroundings. I have seen tiny rivulets of water issuing from a semicircular red sandstone cliff in Zion National Park that created as awe-inspiring a scene as Yosemite Falls, with its millions of gallons a minute and tremendous drop. The particular "falls" in Zion occurred within a natural amphitheater with a cool, leafy glade at its base and a "weeping wall' on the cliff face, covered with maidenhair ferns, pentstemon, and other delicate plants, which—in the midst of an area of rock, aridity, and tough plants—created a delightfully unexpected fantasy realm. Yosemite Falls, by contrast, is visible from a long distance and does not present the same sort of surprise at close range.

THE AUDITORY QUALITY OF WATER

Water produces an endless range of sounds as it flows over and around obstructions, as it sprays into the air and then returns to the surface, as it falls over rocks into pools, as it pulls air into its fold and combines with it to produce even greater nuances in white water and waves. I seriously doubt that any of the sounds created by water could be considered distressing or annoying—except for flood waters or the waves accompanying a hurricane! Poorly located fountains, however, can create an unacceptable level of noise for surrounding offices or shops.

As a resident both of the rainy Pacific Northwest and of the arid Southwest I have experienced very different attitudes toward water and its sounds. In hot, dry climates such as parts of California, Spain, and Mexico the sound of water, whether at the "tinkling" level or at the roaring level, has a different effect upon the observer than it does in a wetter climate, but I should add, however, that, even though the residents of Seattle and Portland are accustomed to the unrelenting sound of falling water for about eight months of the year, their cities have some of the most interesting and inventive water features in the United States. In the "dry season," at least, these fountains provide a delightful range of effects and sounds and are more readily accessible to people than many found in more "corporate" settings in eastern cities. A psychological case can be made that the very sound of water has a cooling effect upon people in a hot climate. Even if the source is not apparent, the sound creates a sense of anticipation and is an attracting force.

THE FEEL OF WATER

Fountain designers are often plagued by clients who are overly concerned about people actually getting *into* the water and leaving them liable for damage suits in case of injury. Anyone who hikes through a hot woodland or on a rocky mountain trail experiences the same urge upon arriving at a stream, pool, or waterfall that a city worker experiences upon discovering a cool, splashing urban fountain after trudging the hot sidewalks on a summer day. The natural urge is to proceed beyond the visual and auditory experiences: to look and to listen is often not sufficient to satisfy our deepest needs. We want to *feel* the water in order to complete our experience of it. In the mountains we are free to take off our clothes, duck our heads in the water, drink it, swim in it, do what we want with it. The supreme frustration in the city—and not just for children—is to be told to stay out of fountains and pools, and this situation has been intelligently met only in recent years.

The most notable innovations in the area of participatory public water features began in the early 60s with Lawrence Halprin's Lovejoy and Auditorium Forecourt fountains in Portland, Oregon, both of which were conceived from the very beginning as places to encourage freedom and interplay of observer and water. Throughout this study I point out other significant attempts by urban designers to maximize the potential for various means of contact with water, including some that allow the participant/observer to control the water flow.

WATER IN REPOSE

In quiet ponds, lagoons, canals, or lakes water presents an entirely different set of moods, sounds, and settings than water in motion. Water in repose is usually associated with meditation, contemplation, poetry, and music; a setting for love or laziness; a time and place for recharging—minimum-energy activities that reflect the low energy of the water. A rock dropped into still water creates ripples that continue to spread for some distance, an effect too tantalizing for children or adults to resist.

The certainty that all water in repose has another personality, waiting to be awakened, to alter its entire character, is brought out by Hubbard and Kimball in their classic *Landscape Design:* "More than any other element in a landscape composition, a lake or pond surface is a unified thing. It is all of the same material, sharply contrasted with its surroundings; it lies all at the same level, and it has from its motion, the sound of its waves, its constant play and change under the influence of wind and current, a life and character which is almost a personality. In its responsiveness to the forces of wind and storm, in the suddenness with which it may pass from calm to gaiety to gloom or fury, its range in emotional effect is so great as to make it, in this respect, a thing apart from the other elements of landscape except perhaps the sky."

It is quite refreshing to read descriptions of this sort in an era in which many environmental designers are becoming programmed, like their computers, to perceive only numerical values in such features as streams and lakes. Such writings provide a more profound link with and understanding of natural phenomena than the very best of the computerized resource analyses now in vogue. It's quite possible that not only our ability to describe but also our level of sensitivity has become attenuated. Since the trend to pseudoscientific quantification of the unquantifiable has spread into many fields, it accomplishes little to bemoan the fact. I still maintain that Chinese landscape artists, early poets, and landscape writers such as Hubbard and Kimball are better able to communicate, in their respective mediums, the character and quality of water in nature than the best of the resource analysts of today.

1-1. Water in Repose: Redwood River, Minnesota.

WATER AS SCULPTOR

Water has created monumental sculptural environments that man will never equal. In the Sierra Nevada, the Grand Canyon, the Utah canyons, the limestone channels and caverns of the Ohio Valley and the Appalachians, and many other places water has carved rock into infinite forms and textures, limited only by the nature and hardness of the material.

In many parts of the Southwest one encounters long, sculptured channels in sandstone with concave depressions, hanging shelves, and flowing lines—but with no water! They are created by seasonal water, which disappears for most of the year, only to periodically reappear and continue the unending production of rock sculpture that is never finished but always evolving. In other areas sandstone, a very porous rock, discharges stored water from a large area along a seam, which then becomes a "weeping wall" that supports many types of moisture-loving plants.

The rock sculpture produced by water in granitic areas such as the Sierra Nevada in California has an entirely different character from that produced in sandstone and other sedimentary areas. In the Sierra much of the original sculpting was accomplished by ice in the form of glacial movements. The boulders that were left behind then became the sculpting tools as they themselves changed shape, crashing and rubbing against other rocks and against the solid granite stream beds. Here is possibly the greatest variety of water sounds and sights to be found in any one part of the United States; any particular half-mile stretch of stream bed possesses more beauty of sculptural form than one could hope to find anywhere else. Many visitors have felt themselves permanently transformed after experiencing the almost mystical purity and beauty of the Sierran rocks and streams. Much of the granitic rock found throughout the western mountains is basically light gray in color with flecks of black mica. The transformation that this type of rock undergoes when wet, especially in the crystal water of a mountain stream, is truly amazing. It becomes as rich as a finely woven tapestry beneath the stream, and, as the light changes, it often assumes a transparent emerald tone. Many of the excellent Sierra Club publications beautifully illustrate the magnificence of these rocks and water.

1-2, 1-3, and 1-4. Water-sculpted sandstone channel, Utah.

1-5. Natural fountain, Sierra Nevada, California.

1-6. Mountain stream in granite, Sierra Nevada, California.

2. HISTORY OF WATER IN DESIGN

EGYPT AND MESOPOTAMIA

Little is known of very early gardens or decorative uses of water, as they are the very elements that alter the most over time and that survive for the shortest period in comparison to architecture, tombs, sculpture, and other archaeological remains. Egyptian gardens were pictured in tombs, in sculptural relief, and in paintings, so we do know that decorative ponds and canals, many of which doubled as irrigation channels or storage ponds, were constructed. The designs were invariably formal and geometric and in that sense the prototype for garden and water-basin designs in Europe and the Near East. Some private Egyptian villas apparently utilized decorative pools for practical purposes such as raising fish for food. Many of these pools were T-shaped and contained plants such as lotus and papyrus, easily identifiable in paintings of the era.

Faced with the unique set of problems posed by their rivers, Mesopotamian engineers created a vast network of lakes, reservoirs, and canals, which were destroyed, restored by Nebuchadnezzar between 604 and 561 B.C., then destroyed again by Persian invaders. Probably the earliest known carved decorative water basin, the ancient Lagash, was found at Tello and is thought to date from 3,000 B.C. The Babylonians and Assyrians are known from ancient writings to have constructed garden ponds similar in style to the Egyptian basins. One of the most fascinating gardens in history, if we are to believe the Greek historians Strabo and Diodorus, were the Hanging Gardens of Babylon. Created by Nebuchadnezzar on a terraced structure to please a Persian wife about 605 B.C., they almost certainly contained intricate irrigation conduits and decorative fountains. Diodorus mentions "certain engines" to draw "plenty of water out of the river Euphrates, through certain conduits hid from the spectator, which supplied it to the platform of the garden." Since the accounts of the Greek historians were derived from word-of-mouth descriptions passed down over many generations, we can only surmise the technical sophistication of such a system. Given their known achievements in hydraulics, however, we can assume a very high-level quality of technical design for a project under royal mandate.

GREECE AND ROME

In Greece we find firm evidence of the existence of numerous fountains that combined utilitarian, religious, and aesthetic functions. The original meaning of the word "fountain" refers to a spring of water. In Greece many of these springs were dedicated to gods, goddesses, nymphs, and heroes. A planted grove or temple was often located at the spring, and the water was conducted into carved basins, often incorporating sculpture. These fountains served as sources of drinking water and often included a structure to cover and enclose the draw basin. One fountain in Corinth reportedly featured a statue of the horse Pegasus with water flowing from its hooves. Another Corinthian fountain included a bronze statue of Neptune standing upon a dolphin from which the water flowed. A wide range of mystical, medicinal, and other qualities were ascribed to various fountains.

What began as sacred springs, with various legends, properties, and gods, goddesses, or nymphs associated with each, developed into more elaborate covered and piped fountains, often with temples built nearby. Pausanias, who traveled through Greece about A.D. 150, described many of these fountains in detail; he stated that no place deserved to be called a "city" that did not possess a major fountain. The earliest architecturally developed spring on record was the Callirrhoe in Athens, built around 560–510 B.C. The water was directed into nine outlets, which consisted of bronze lion heads with water issuing from the mouths.

The Hellenistic civilization, which began with Alexander the Great, produced many brilliant and remarkable cities with pressurized water systems, aqueducts, town squares, and undoubtedly ingenious fountains about which we unfortunately know little. Cities such as Alexander, Antioch, Pergamum, Ephesus, and others provided the Romans with prototypes from which they adopted many of their best ideas and forms.

Mechanical devices associated with fountains, which provide whimsical touches, practical jokes, or music from water organs, are usually associated with Renaissance Italy, but many originated in Hellenistic Greece and were described and illustrated in the *Pneumatica* by Hero of Alexandria. He illustrated the opening of temple doors with steam generated by a boiler; birds that whistled by means of compressed air, which was also used to make figures move and trumpets to blow; and the water organ. The basic prinicples of these devices were all developed in detail on paper by the Greeks. Whether any of them were constructed we have no way of knowing. There is no reason, however, given the particular genius of the Hellenistic Greeks, to assume that some of these devices were not constructed as working models at the very least. Renaissance architects merely revived these devices after rediscovering them in ancient literature: they did not invent them, as is so commonly assumed. Hero described in detail a very complex hydraulic organ and a device in which singing and turning birds were operated by pulleys, siphons, and compressed air, which was the prototype for that constructed at the Villa d'Este in the 16th century.

When we speak of Rome as a city of fountains, we are really talking about relatively few fountains, virtually all of which are of Renaissance or later vintage. Modern Rome is but a shadow of her former self in terms of abundance of fountains and other water features. Ancient Rome was adorned with 1,212 public fountains, 11 great Imperial thermae, and 926 public baths at the time of the first Gothic sacking of the city. Only 5 of the original fountains still exist today. Many of the original fountains were adorned with statuary by Greek sculptors, and their plentitude and magnificence amazed all early observers. The proliferation of public as well as private fountains was a direct result of the aqueduct system, which brought incredible quantities of water into the city from springs and mountain streams. Each aqueduct terminated in a *castellum*, or massive display fountain, which was inscribed with the name of the emperor or other benefactor responsible. As statuary was commonly used as decoration for these fountains, many of the castelli were named after the statues, such as the Fountain of the Shepherd, the Fountain of Orpheus, and the Fountain of the Three Masks. The fountain of Marfario, the river god, in the courtyard of the Capitoline Museum is still in existence. One of the ancient fountains, called the Meta Sudans, was a tall, cone-shaped structure near the Colosseum that dripped water from holes in its side, lending the appearance of a "sweating goalpost." Even today many of the existing aqueducts feed fountains scattered around the city. For many centuries after the sacking of Rome in A.D. 410 the aqueducts and the water features they served fell into ruin or were vandalized. Of all the many products of civili-

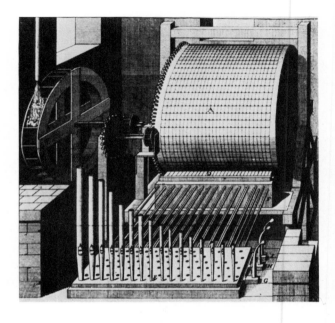

2-1. Engraving of a water organ from Stephen Switzer's *An Introduction to a General System of Hydrostaticks and Hydraulics, Philosophical and Practical,* London, 1729.

zation the public fountain has proven to be one of the most susceptible to destruction. When the aqueducts ceased to flow, the fountains seemed to have no purpose and were removed, as in many other cultures that underwent invasion or revolution.

A number of Roman aristocrats and rulers built lavish villas outside Rome to escape the summer heat and congestion, and many of these contained both pools and fountains fed with lead pipes. Hadrian's villa at Tivoli, constructed from 125 to 136 A.D., included a vast complex of baths, a colonnaded pool, a marble nymphaeum, decorative canals, and a circular water theater with a central island embellished with planting and courts. Pliny describes what seems to be an irrigation system: "Next each seat is a little fountain; and throughout the whole hippodrome small rills conveyed through pipes run murmuring along, wheresoever the hand of art has seen proper to conduct them; watering here and there different spots of verdure, and in their progress bathing the whole." Gardening and ornamental horticulture had reached a pinnacle of development by Pliny's time, and he describes the creation of the lawn and other plantings in some detail. Hothouses with mica windows were apparently used for propagation and forcing of blooms, and gardeners were held in esteem.

2-2. Fountain of Marfario, the river god, Rome.

ISLAMIC CULTURES

For all the visual excitement, opulence, grandness of scale, and whimsy of Italian Renaissance water features, I must confess a greater respect for the Islamic use of water. While the Renaissance fountains were possible only at a certain time and in a certain place, fed by a plentitude of mountain streams and springs, the Islamic manner of using a minimum amount of water to maximum advantage has been successfully used in India, Pakistan, the Middle East, northern Africa, Spain, and Portugal.

2-4. Pool in the Grand Court of the Royal Mosque, Isfahan. (Photo courtesy H. Roger-Viollet, Paris.)

Persia

Whether in ancient Persia, Moorish Spain, or North Africa water was a central feature of garden design, with religious symbolism; it defined space and interpenetrated from the open court into the enclosure. The Islamic view of Heaven, or Paradise, is a beautiful garden, and the Day of Judgment will take place in gardens of pleasure complete with cooling springs and fountains. The traditional Persian garden was composed of four essentials: water for irrigation, display, and sound; shade trees for shelter; flowers for scent and color; and music to delight the ears. A typical garden design found from Persia to Spain and in many old carpets and miniature paintings is a quadrant pattern with water channels dividing the garden into four sections. There was usually a pool or small hill with a pavilion at the intersection of the channels.

Persian culture did not wither with the Mongolian invasions of the 13th and 14th centuries, and, when the Mongols invaded northern India, they created many beautiful Persian-style gardens in present-day Afghanistan and India. In the Vale of Kashmir, blessed with an abundance of mountain springs for a water supply, the Moguls created some of the most famous gardens in history in an unsurpassed setting. The water was usually contained in a great tank or holding pond and channeled down through the various levels of terraced gardens into rectangular pools with jets in

2-3. Water-channel maze, Palace at Meknes, Morocco.

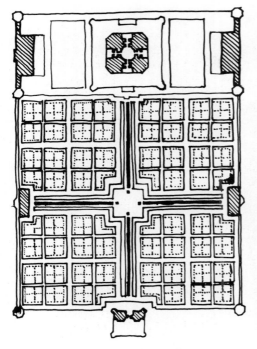

2-5. Plan of Taj Mahal gardens.

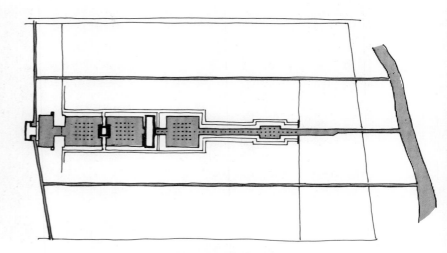

2-6. Plan of water features at Achibal.

the shape of lotus buds. Marble pavilions were often built over the channels so that the water flowing beneath kept the floors cool. In the famous Shalimar garden on Lake Dal there are four terraces within a walled space; each terrace had a particular function. One was the emperor's personal garden; another, called the Abode of Love, was used by the Empress and her court. A black marble pavilion stood in the center in a large pool with 140 fountains. A common feature of these gardens, later utilized in Renaissance Italy, was a sloped water chute, called a *chadar,* which had a textured, fretted surface to break the water flow into a more turbulent, foaming pattern. It was constructed on a slope rather than vertically in order to produce more reflective sparkle from the sun.

The majority of the gardens of the Mogul emperors no longer exist, since their water supply has been turned to the more practical tasks of agricultural irrigation, but several in addition to the Shalimar are worth mentioning. The water palaces along the shores of Lake Dal were called *baghs;* one of the greatest is Nishat Bagh, a walled garden that originally had twelve terraces. With a series of falls and quiet pools that descend to the Lake, the water in Nishal Bagh was also channeled to serve the flower beds. In the eastern Kashmir plain, somewhat remote from the main center of Kashmiri Mughal gardens around Lake Dal, are two more gardens of interest, Achibal and Verinag. Both are 17th-century water gardens in which the water is still in use. In Achibal one finds an extravagant display of water by Persian standards in the form of a great

cascade at least 70′ in width. This garden was also one of the first to use lighting on water for decorative purposes. There are similar descriptions of the use of lights in conjunction with some of the Italian Renaissance fountains, so it is obvious that fountain lighting was *not* introduced with electricity!

The typical Persian garden consisted of rigid geometric divisions with relatively level terraces, all interlaced with a network of irrigation and ornamental water channels above the flower beds, which received their water from spaced outlets in the channels. A second Shalimar Bagh, constructed at Lahore in 1634, resembles the Taj Mahal garden in both general layout and specific details, leading some authorities to speculate that the same architect was responsible for both. Even the interior design of the Taj Mahal resembles the garden designs in layout, lending credence to the view that Mughal gardens and parts are connected much more closely in design to the buildings than is the case anywhere in Europe. At Feria Bagh, another Mughal waterside palace, there existed a superb system of water supply and sewage, with the piping-system layout repeating the building plan. An exact drawing of the building shows the complete system. The palace featured a fountain in the center, which drew water from the lake that surrounded it. Conduits under the floor carried water in four directions to smaller basins in the ancillary rooms, and from these rooms the water ran on to large reservoirs outside the palace.

2-7. Court of the Oranges *(Patio de los Naranjos)*, Seville.

Spain

It is difficult to discuss the superb Moorish palaces and water features in isolation from the other remarkable achievements of the culture. Christian culture at the time was stagnant and uncreative by comparison: its greatest architectural monuments do not measure up to the Mosque at Cordoba or the Alhambra in Granada. The Moors reintroduced high-level hydraulics and irrigation systems, constructing elaborate cisterns and reservoirs, developing luxurious vineyards and terraces, and, of course, building some of the most magnificent structures in the history of man.

Water, both seen and heard, was more indispensable to garden design in Moorish Spain than plant material. Both the scarcity of supply and the cultural style that the Moors brought with them to Spain influenced their technique of making a small amount of water appear to be a great deal. Water was confined to small channels or narrow pools, with no waste allowed to escape unused: conduits ran from tree to tree for irrigation. There were very few hidden water courses: all channels were open and visible whenever possible. Basins were designed to be continually full to the brim, with water overflowing the edges into a secondary channel. The basins were often faceted or carved in a lotus pattern, which makes a small volume of water seem greater. Water was "used with due regardful thrift," as one observer put it.

The Moors also developed the art of painting tiles, which were used on walls, floors, and pools with such a captivating effect that it has been copied to this day.

2-8. Glazed-tile fountain, Maria Luisa Park, Seville.

2-9. Alcazar gardens, Seville.

Even after the expulsion of the Moors from the Iberian peninsula by the Christians their artistic achievements were so admired by the Catholic Spaniards that they retained many Moorish artisans and architects to develop some of their own buildings and gardens, which resulted in what is known as the Mudejar style, a blending of Moorish and Christian design. The Alcazar at Seville, constructed a hundred years after the Moorish occupation ended, is a product of this intermingling.

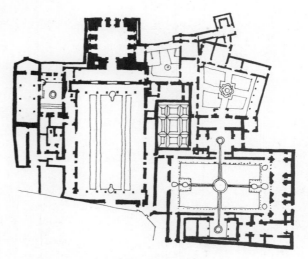

2-10. Plan of the Alhambra.

Although there are numerous Islamic palaces in the Middle East that offer good examples of the Moors' ingenious yet conservative use of water, the most familiar to tourists is the Alhambra on Sabika Hill in Granada, Spain. In 1238 Mohammed ben Alhamar began developing this fortress-palace by bringing in water from the River Darro through a system of reservoirs, cisterns, aqueducts, and pipes to a large storage tank within the walls of the Alhambra complex itself. In the midst of this superb setting, with the Sierra Nevada as a backdrop, the Nasrid Dynasty, which ruled the Kingdom of Granada, apparently underwent a transformation that softened their religious fanaticism and warlike tendencies into a flowering of art and poetry. The superb quality of Arabic calligraphy lent itself to bas-relief inscriptions of poetry on walls, vessels, fountain basins, and other surfaces, giving the decorated surface an incredible richness: one often doesn't realize that the surface consists of words at all, so beautifully interwoven is the calligraphy with the surrounding motif and pattern. Throughout the Alhambra are found exquisitely detailed bas-relief carvings and plasterwork, which have defied their fragility for seven centuries; the ceilings are so intricate in faceting that they present an appearance not unlike a view through a kaleidoscope.

2-11 and 2-12. Court of the Lions, Alhambra.

2-13. Court of the Myrtles, Alhambra.

2-14. Stone source basin, Court of the Myrtles, Alhambra.

In the Court of the Lions is a profoundly proportioned space enclosed by finely carved alabaster columns, often in groups of two and four, which have been compared to a grove of 124 palm trees. Water bubbles up through bronze heads into circular basins set into the floor of the enclosed spaces on all four sides and is then carried in narrow channels over marble steps and into the central basin, which is fed by its own water supply. Water flows from each of four directions towards the center in the classical Islamic pattern that is seen in Persian gardens. The effects of this use of water are manifold and full of unexpected surprises. In one of the rooms the water bubbles into a floor-level basin, and the entire ceiling, with all its intricate faceting, is reflected mirrorlike in the basin from a certain angle, a display that was certainly intended by the designer.

The Royal Baths of the Alhambra are in remarkably good condition and are truly a delight to experience. Wall, floors, and benches are totally covered with intricate tile designs in gold, red, green, and blue; soft light filters through clerestory stained glass above, and the whole effect is quite magical. Following the Roman plan, the baths offered cold, hot, and steam baths: the frigidarium, tepidarium, and calvarium. The Baths originally had a huge copper boiler from which lead and copper ducts ran through the floors and walls to the four sections. The floors are of white marble with central drainage channels.

The Alhambra is by no means representative of Moorish architecture in Spain: it was rather a late and rare expression of a culture that underwent considerable transformation, internecine warfare, and architectural evolution, culminating in the Nasrid style. The majority of palaces and other buildings from earlier periods of Moorish rule have unfortunately not survived. Luckily, however, the Alhambra complex has endured remarkably intact for seven hundred years, suffering occupations and bombardments, vandalism and centuries of neglect.

2-15. Partal gardens, Alhambra.

2-16. Pool, Partal Gardens, Alhambra.

The Alhambra is one of the best remaining examples of Moorish architecture, but there are numerous descriptions of earlier palaces in Cordoba and elsewhere that were probably even more elaborate but that are now gone. Cordoba is thought to have been constructed over a vast area that contained a half-million people at its pinnacle, but not one of the many Moorish palaces remains. Abd al-Rahman the Great, responsible for much of the Moorish construction in Cordoba, built a combination fortress-country mansion called Medina Azzahra, a veritable city in scale (280 acres), outside Cordoba. Marble and other stones were brought from quarries in Carthage, Tunis, Rome, Constantinople, and Spain; descriptions of the number of workmen, the construction funds, and the lavishness of the architecture led many observers to feel that they were exaggerated myths, but excavations in recent years have confirmed these accounts.

Remarkable fountains of gilt bronze and green marble had been shipped from Constantinople, and one incredibly elegant room, the Salon de los Califas, apparently possessed walls and a ceiling of gold and multicolored marble blocks. There are descriptions of a large quicksilver-filled pool in the center of this room. Eight doors decorated with gold and ebony stood between piers of colored marble and clear crystal. When the sun shone into this room, the effect was blinding; the Caliph would astonish his visitors by disturbing the pool of quicksilver, causing the entire room to be filled with moving reflections.

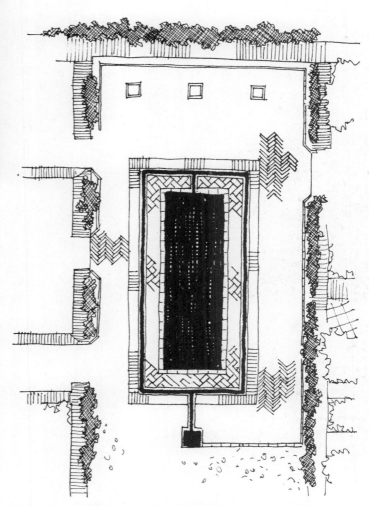

2-17. Plan of the pool in the Partal Gardens. Water from the square basin traverses the perimeter of the pool in a narrow channel, reentering at the opposite end of the basin.

Another innovation that the rest of Europe would not discover for many centuries was the installation of running water in the city's latrines. Although Cordoba possesses fine remains of earlier structures of the Romans, Goths, and other civilizations, the Moors improved the city immensely with their public gardens, fountains, water system, public baths, and buildings.

2-19. Court of the Oranges, Seville.

2-18. The use of water channels to irrigate trees.

The Moors developed the ingenious method of directing irrigation water to trees in courtyard gardens through interconnected surface channels, a detail now common throughout Spain. Water flows in little stone-edged channels that run from tree to tree and can be controlled with small wooden dams, inserted as necessary to channel or cut off water in a particular portion of the courtyard.

Islamic fountain basins were invariably mounted close to the ground, often barely extending above the surface of the surrounding plane. Whether this was merely an extension of the need to place fountains used for purposes of ablution low or whether it was derived from the aesthetics afforded to people using cushions on the floor rather than furniture is difficult to say. The basins are generally circular and shallow, sometimes scalloped in a lotus-flower pattern, sometimes in an angular pattern, and usually carved from marble and other fine-grained stones. They are thought to have served the function of cooling the courts in which they were placed through evaporation in addition to their religious functions, which explains the large surface-area-to-volume ratio. Their simplicity and fine proportions were appreciated by the later Christian rulers, who commonly raised them up on Renaissance pedestals into the typical candelabra shape later found all over Europe and America. Some authorities theorized that the basins were raised in order to be better seen and appreciated; the custom probably reflected both the different function played by the fountain and the different architectural and cultural tastes of the Christians. Several fountains in the Alhambra, including the Lions Fountain, have been restored during the last decades to their original Moorish designs, with the Renaissance additions removed.

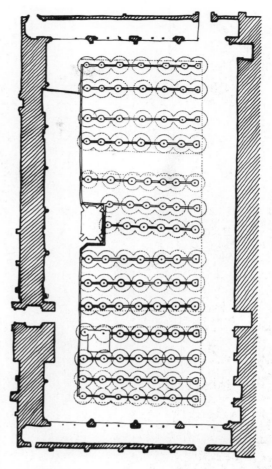

2-20. Plan of the Court of the Oranges in Cordoba, illustrating the network of irrigation channels running from tree to tree.

2-21. Marble basin, Alhambra.

2-22. Generalife gardens, Granada.

2-23. Cooling jets springing from the paving. Alcazar Gardens, Seville. (Photo courtesy H. Roger-Viollet, Paris.)

The Generalife was the summer residence and park of the Sultans of Granada, and, though it has been added to by successive generations, it still maintains its original combination of hidden water courts and open vistas across the ravine to the Alhambra below. A number of ingenious uses of water are found in these gardens, some of which were later copied several centuries later in Italian Renaissance gardens. The Italian Ambassador Andrea Navaggiero, who lived in Granada after the Christian reconquest, gives an exact description of the Generalife at the time. "It has many patios, all of which are well provided with water. One of them in particular is traversed by a channel of running water, edged with extremely fine myrtles and orange trees. . . . Water runs throughout the palace, even into the very rooms, making it a most pleasant spot in summer. In addition, in one courtyard that is completely filled with foliage, where a meadow has been made by planting some trees, there is a contrivance of hidden taps by which the water is suddenly turned on, to the surprise of the person in the meadow, and the water springs and gurgles forth, rising to drench him completely. The water can be turned off equally unobtrusively. Above this spot, in another garden, there is a wide, handsome staircase and a small platform, in which a certain flagstone is the source of all the water that runs through the palace. There it is enclosed by many sluices, so that it can be turned on when desired. The staircase is made in such a way that on every so many steps there is a plateau with a central cavity into which the water can be diverted. The stone balustrades on each side of the staircase also have concave stones on top, which act as water-channels." These staircase-water channels still exist, as does a central water canal with arching jets lining both sides, a style found in later Spanish gardens.

The key to the Islamic garden, especially in contrast to later Renaissance and baroque gardens and parks, is its essentially spiritual, poetic, and contemplative purpose, completely opposed in nature to the social, ceremonial, classical-inspired play areas of the Italian and French aristocracy. Lacking a distinction between religious and civil life, spiritual motives and purposes pervaded every aspect of Islamic existence, including its gardens. The western garden or park cuts through and overcomes nature, opening out broad vistas and avenues. The Arabic park, by contrast, secludes its spaces in hidden courts, with only subtle enframed vistas of distant areas here and there.

The other palaces and gardens above the Generalife—and all over southern Spain—disappeared when the water supply dried up or ceased to be maintained. Luckily, the water still runs in the Alhambra and the Generalife—and we are able to experience at least a glimpse of this noble civilization.

RENAISSANCE AND BAROQUE EUROPE

With the Renaissance, which began in the 14th century, came a humanistic revival of classical influence that affected all aspects of life: it produced a flowering of the arts, a fresh but classically influenced architecture, and modern science.

Even the water displays of the Renaissance illustrated the return to classical Greek and Roman symbolism and ideas, for, as is mentioned in the section on Greek fountains, the Greeks were completely familiar with the whimsical, mechanical devices such as whistling birds and water organs that are usually attributed to Renaissance designers and inventors. Although there are no physical remains of such mechanical water devices in Greece, there is no evidence that none was ever constructed there, as these contraptions were largely made of wood and therefore have not survived in the Renaissance gardens either. What is fairly certain is that, coincident with the revival of interest in classical literature, poetry, symbolism, and architectural proportions, was a rediscovery of Hellenistic writings and hydraulic inventions such as those described in the *Pneumatica* by Hero. The devices described in minute detail by Montaigne and other writers are almost exact reproductions of the devices described in Hero's book.

In contrast to the medieval era, in which the entire culture was influenced by religion and religious symbolism, the Renaissance glorified secular art—and, in fact, in the process destroyed a tremendous quantity of fine medieval art. In the Renaissance the emphasis shifted from that of man serving God within a religious community to one in which man became individualized, more engrossed in trade, city life, and private pleasures. This style of life, with its affinity to Hellenistic Greece and pre-Christian Rome, was accompanied by the development of vast private country villas, a reestablishment of a pattern of living common in Roman times. Huge storehouses of classical Roman and Greek statues were continually being unearthed as the fascination with the arts and literature of that era grew. Many fountains were constructed in city squares and private villas merely by assembling classical statuary and combining it with a sarcophagus to serve as a basin.

Because styles in architecture and painting were continually changing during the Renaissance, there is no clearly defined entrance into the baroque period.

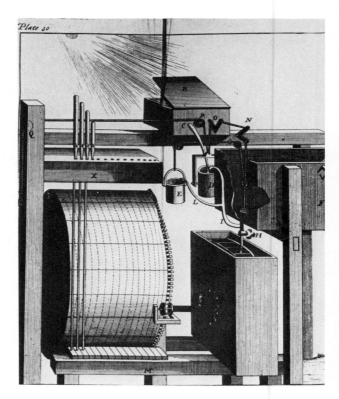

2-24. Engraving of a water-organ mechanism from Stephen Switzer's *An Introduction to a General System of Hydrostaticks and Hydraulics, Philosophical and Practical,* London, 1729.

Some historians claim that the golden age of the Renaissance ended by 1520 and that the beginnings of the baroque are evident by 1580. Others date it with the development of a lighter and gayer architectural style, such as that of Bernini, around 1630.

Renaissance gardens were usually typified by a strict, regimented formality of layout, with different parts of the garden divided from one another in a tectonic setting. Renaissance designers generally accepted the natural terrain and made no significant attempt to alter it or impose order upon it. Baroque gardens, however, made generous use of ramps, terraces, and steps, which gave an overall unity lacking in the Renaissance to the various elements of the garden. Baroque gardens were laid out on an axis that respected the alignment of the architecture; they were symmetrically arranged, with every detail determined by its relation to the whole. Most of the villas that contain significant water displays are products of the baroque spirit and of the utilization of complex hydraulics to make available massive quantities of water. Fountains in Renaissance gardens and squares usually featured only trickles of water, while gushing volumes of water typified the later baroque parks and villas.

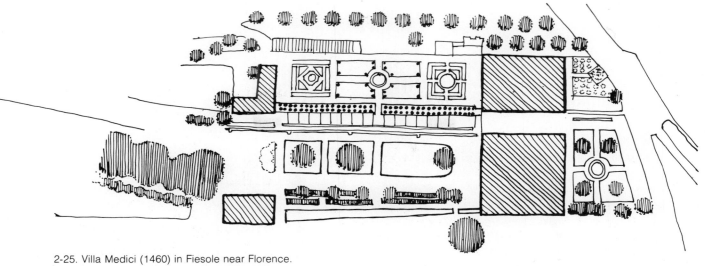

2-25. Villa Medici (1460) in Fiesole near Florence.

2-26. Vista toward water cascades, Villa Garzoni, Collodi.

There were also many variations of style and design from one part of Italy to another as a result of the personal tastes of the patrons, availability of water, and other influences. For example, the fountains of Florence were primarily figure sculptures with a sparse use of water, which reflected both the severely limited supply (mostly from wells) and also the local Tuscan emphasis on high-quality figure sculpture. The more architectonic Roman fountains seem to have been designed primarily for the display of water and are rather awkward when dry or inoperative; the Florentine fountains, on the other hand, existed to display the sculpture. An excellent example is the Tribolo Fountain of the Labyrinth, a three-tiered basin fountain surmounted with Giambologna's sculptured figure of *Florence Rising from the Waters*. This figure represents a woman wringing out her long hair; water descends in a fine stream from her hair into the basin, from which it emerges through faces on the underside to descend to a lower basin and thence to the main basin at ground level.

This general style of fountain, with basins mounted in tiers and surmounted by a work of sculpture, became a rather rigid prototype that persisted well into the present century. Fountains of this candelabra type may be seen in parks and gardens across the United States. The most original contribution of Renaissance and baroque gardens was probably the man-made cascade in which massive volumes of water are carried through stylized channels; over ramps, boulders, and walls; into basins and out of mouths; sometimes transported in this controlled way down an entire hillside. Some of the most extensive cascades are located at the following villas: Villa Aldobrandini at Frascati (1560), Villa Lante at Bagnaia (1566), Villa Torlonia at Frascata (1600s), Villa Garzoni at Collodi (1652), and Palazzo Reale, Caserta (1752).

As the influence of the Italian Renaissance and baroque style spread throughout Europe, many cascades were constructed in other countries. A Frenchman named Grillet designed the Great Cascade at Chatsworth, Derbyshire, England in 1696. Another Frenchman, Le Blond, designed extensive water features with cascades for Peter the Great at Peterhof, near Leningrad, Russia. Guernieri designed a massive baroque cascade around 1700 for the castle of Wilhelmshohe at Kassel, Germany. It was 35' wide and almost 800' long, which represented only a third of the originally intended length!

2-27. Water channel at Villa Lante, Bagnaia.

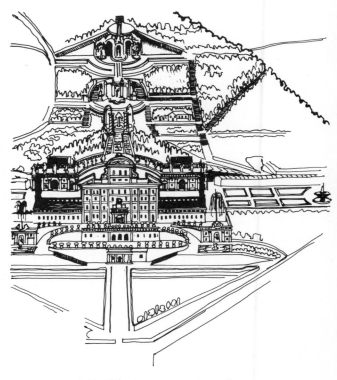

2-28. Villa Aldobrandini, Frascati.

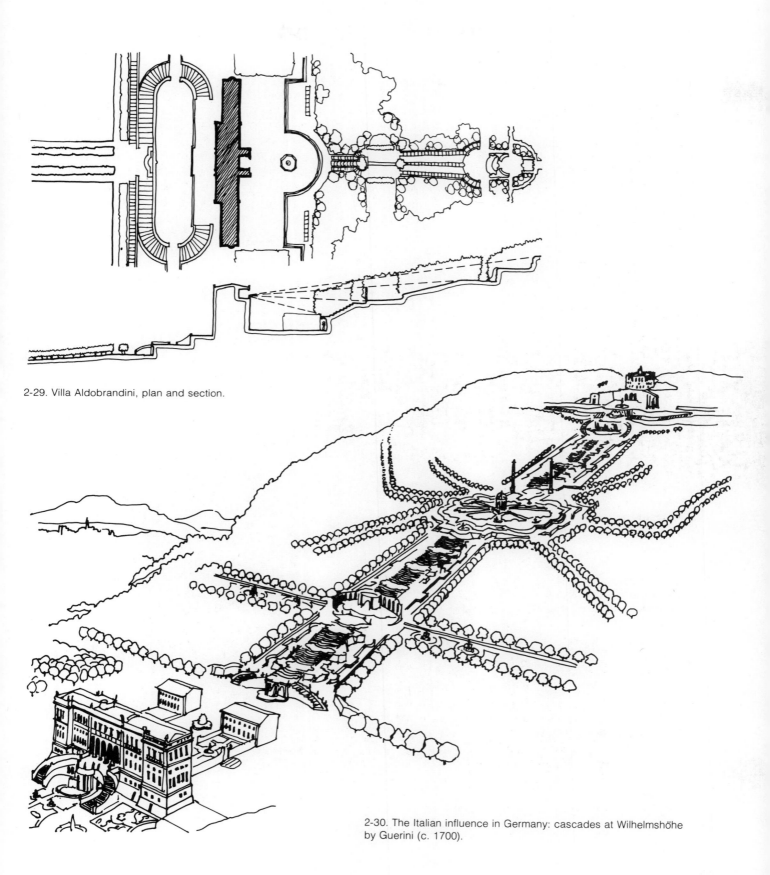

2-29. Villa Aldobrandini, plan and section.

2-30. The Italian influence in Germany: cascades at Wilhelmshöhe by Guerini (c. 1700).

The last major Italian-baroque water display is an example of a style that was exported, added to, and brought back to its original home in an altered state. The Palazzo Reale is probably the largest decorative water display ever built, and it combines the Italian cascade with Spanish and French influences. It was designed in 1752 by Luigi Vanvitelli for Charles III, a grandson of Louis XIV and son of King Philip of Spain. With a main vista 2 miles in length, it features a long cascade that is transformed into a water staircase that culminates in a French canal. The statuary is very similar to that of Versailles, and the entire design was obviously influenced by the French example.

It is worth examining the wide range of whimsical devices used with water displays in Renaissance and baroque gardens, as it illustrates a much lighter and more informal use than we might imagine in seeing only the fountains that still exist. The parks and palace gardens of the period that followed were certainly designed more for pomp and ceremony than for individual delights. Some fascinating and ingenious uses of water created a whole world of sounds and surprises, from the hissing of a stone lioness and the horn of a centaur to a playable water organ that utilized compressed air and water to create musical sounds. There was also a fountain called the Owl Fountain, designed by G. del Luca, which featured twittering bronze birds that were silenced at regular intervals by a shrieking owl; this invention was modeled on the previously mentioned water-driven device described by Hero in *Pneumatica.* Claude Venard, a Frenchman, is credited with the design of the water organ at the Villa d'Este, but he was obviously familiar with Greek descriptions of such devices. Trick benches and hidden jets were common in these villa gardens and were used to surprise casual visitors. It is clear that people-participation fountains are hardly an invention of the 20th century! In fact, we have a long way to go to equal the playfulness and individual control and the wealth of sounds and activities associated with baroque water theaters.

CASCATA D'ACQVA, SOPRA IL TEATRO DELLA VILLA ALDOBRANDINA DI BELVEDERE A FRASCATI, CON LE DVE COLONNE CHE VERSA- 'NO ACQVA NELLA SOMMITA, CON VARI GIVOCHI, CHE BAGNANO QVELLI CHE SALGONO LA SCALA PER VEDERE.

2-31. The Water Stairway, Villa Aldobrandini. The columns spout water that travels downward in spiral channels around the face of the columns. (From Falda's *Le Fontane di Roma,* 1675.)

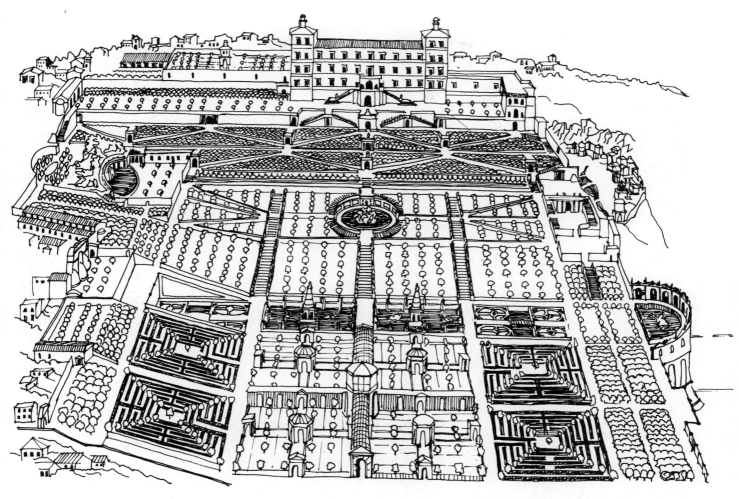

2-32. Villa d'Este, Tivoli in the 17th century.

The Villa d'Este at Tivoli

The Villa de'Este at Tivoli was one of the forerunners of the baroque garden style, encompassing many individual areas that are combined into an architectonic whole, connected with ramps, stairs, and cross axes. The town of Tivoli has been a favored suburban resort of Romans for many centuries. Hadrian's imperial villa, built between 121 and 137 A.D., was a splendid complex of water, gardens, and palace located only a few miles from the Villa d'Este. Cardinal Ippolito II d'Este commissioned the Neapolitan architect Pirro Ligorio to design the Villa de'Este gardens shortly after 1550. Faced with an almost unlimited supply of water from the Aniene River, Ligorio had a tunnel excavated beneath the town that was 600 meters long and over 2 meters in diameter to bring water at a rate of 17,000 gallons per minute into a huge reservoir at the upper end of the gardens.

2-33. The miniature City of Rome backdrop for the outdoor theater, Villa d'Este, Tivoli. (From Falda's *Le Fontane di Roma*, 1675.)

35

2-34. The Hundred Fountains, Villa d'Este, Tivoli.

2-35. Dragon Fountain, Villa d'Este, Tivoli.

2-36 and 2-37. Ovato Fountain, Villa d'Este, Tivoli.

Several hydraulic engineers worked with Ligorio to establish the exact requirements in volume and pressure of the fifty fountains of the villa. Many different architects, engineers, and sculptors worked on individual features within the Villa d'Este complex. Orazio Olivieri was responsible for the Dragon Fountain, which depicts four winged dragons and was designed to commemorate the visit of Pope Gregory XIII. Ligorio himself was responsible for the design of the famous Hundred Fountains, which were originally decorated with stucco that has now disappeared. The Ovato Fountain is probably Ligorio's finest creation. It features a superb waterfall that allows visitors to walk behind and look through. The water flows to the top of the waterfall through a rustic setting of natural rock and sculpted statuary, which acts as a transition from the naturalistic background to the man-made gardens. Another water display recreated ancient Rome in miniature, with small-scale versions of the Pantheon, the Colosseum, and other buildings, and offered an allegorical course of the Aniene into the Tiber and of the Tiber through Rome, complete with Isola Tiberina, an island in the shape of a boat, carrying an obelisk. It was used as a backdrop for an outdoor theater.

2-38. Neptune Fountain, Villa d'Este, Tivoli, constructed in 1927 below the water-organ area.

One of the most impressive water displays in the world is the Neptune Fountain of the Villa d'Este. Although most visitors are not aware of it, this fountain is a relatively new addition to the gardens, having been constructed in 1927. With a perfect balance and harmony of gushing vertical jets and waterfall cascades, this fountain combines both rising and falling water and their accompanying sounds in one majestic display. It was constructed just below the old water-organ fountain, from which one may look down through the Neptune's gushing vertical jets to the old fish-rearing ponds below.

2-39. Original setting below the water organ, Villa d'Este, Tivoli, with naturalistic waterfalls and rockery.

2-40. Stepped water channel, Villa d'Este, Tivoli.

2-41. The Sphinx Fountain, Villa d'Este, Tivoli.

FONTANA DEL SIG. PRENCIPE DI PALLESTRINA
su la Piazza Barberina, alle radici del Quirinale in Via felice, nel Rione di Treui, Architet.a del Cau.Gio·Lorenzo Bernini.
G.B.Falda del·et inc.   G.Iac.Rossi le stampa in Roma alla Pace e Pru·del S.P. 16

2-42. Bernini's Triton Fountain (1642), Rome, with an abundance of water, from Falda's *Le Fontane di Roma,* 1675.

The Fountains of Rome

Since the fountains of Rome are the most widely known in the world and have been copiously described by others, I will offer only brief observations on the subject. The restoration of Rome as a city of fountains was made possible through the repair and restoration of the aqueducts during the Renaissance. The water features of Rome have been lovingly and meticulously documented by H.V. Morton in *The Fountains of Rome,* in which he organizes the various fountains according to the aqueducts that feed them. Morton makes it clear that the Romans were connoisseurs of water quality: individual neighborhoods and fountains alike were extolled because of the particular quality of the aqueduct water that served them.

The Trevi Fountain, a flamboyant and exuberant tableau that seems to erupt from the drab facade of its backdrop building, was widely considered to be a decadent example of bad taste in the last century. In fact, it is more accurately an exciting stage set that has attracted throngs of visitors over the centuries. Although there was an earlier Trevi Fountain dating back

to 1453, the present structure was not completed until the middle of the 18th century on a site slightly removed from the earlier fountain. Both the earlier and the existing fountains represented the termination of the Acqua Vergine. The planning of the existing fountain began in 1640 when Urban VIII asked Bernini to design it. Then followed a series of delays, public protests, and other difficulties that caused Bernini to turn his attention to his other commissions, such as the Triton, the Four Rivers Fountain, and the Bee Fountain. The Trevi Fountain sat in a neglected state, unfinished, for decades after Bernini's death. A new Pope, Clement XII (1730–40), decided to hold a competition for a design. A Frenchman won the competition with his scheme for seven large figures, but the public outcry at awarding the commission to a foreigner caused the Pope to cancel the award. The Pope himself then selected Nocola Salvi, a poet, philosopher, and dilettante, to carry out the Trevi design. This was a period in which vast spectacles were commonplace: massive and complicated stage-set props, fireworks displays, mock ocean battles between small-scale model ships on artificial canals, and other public entertainments

2-43. The Trevi Fountain, Rome, on cleaning day!

were popular. Salvi had himself designed a machine for a fireworks display that had delighted the Romans. The greatest architects of the time were willing to design ephemeral creations that would go up in smoke, as it was the only way to see some of their more fantastic visualizations take form. The work dragged on, even under Salvi, and was unfinished even at this death. The Trevi was finally completed in 1762 under contracts awarded by Clement XIII, the last of fourteen popes who reigned over the 122 years since Urban VII began the tedious process. Salvi wrote a long explanation of the symbolism of the Trevi, which purports to show that the fountain is one great allegory on the nature of water, with Triton, having trouble with his sea-horse, representing the angry ocean; his companion, with a placid "hippocampus," represents the ocean in a tranquil mood. An urn is intended to symbolize the virtues of stored water, and carved trees represent life nourished by water. The Trevi is now electrically pumped and is drained and scrubbed once a week. Workmen in rubber boots retrieve approximately 70,000 lire each week from the basin as a result of the coin-throwing custom, which seems to have begun or to have been revived in the latter part of the 19th century.

2-44 and 2-45. Fountain of the Four Rivers, Rome, by Bernini.

The Fountain of the Four Rivers is generally considered to be Bernini's greatest fountain. He began it in 1648 at the age of fifty and took three years to complete it—with considerable help, of course, from members of his school, who were responsible for sculpting different parts of the fountain. Pope Innocent X, whose family palace was in the Piazza Navona where the fountain was to be located, wanted an obelisk as a central part of the design. Bernini was able to adapt his design to this restriction in an admirable way. There are figures of four giant river gods, representing four rivers and continents: the Danube, the Ganges, the Nile, and the Plate. The water emerges in fine sprays and falls from the rocks beneath the figures, one of which seems to be looking up in amazement at the obelisk. The rock on which these figures rest opens out into a cavelike grotto beneath, in which are located carved creatures that also represent each of the four rivers. The custom of flooding the entire piazza to create a lake began shortly after the completion of the Four Rivers Fountain and gave rise to incredible spectacles with carriages, horses, mules, and children all thronging through the water. A number of engravings show the flooded piazza, a custom that apparently continued until the pavement level was raised in 1867.

2-46. Fountain of the Tortoises, Rome.

2-47. Bernini fountain, St. Peter's Square, Rome.

The Fountain of the Tortoises, the most Florentine of all the Roman fountains, is to many people the most beautiful in Rome. The sculptor was a Florentine named Landini who worked under Jocopo della Porta and completed the fountain in 1584. Unlike most of the fountains in Rome, the figures are of bronze. The original conception was to place dolphins in the upraised hands of the four youths, but this was never carried out. The tortoises were added seventy years later and give the fountain the lightest and most playful character of any to be found in Rome.

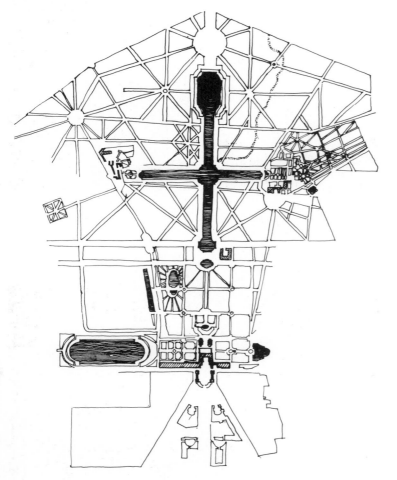

2-48. Plan of Versailles.

Versailles and Vaux-le-Vicomte

Although the French were never able to recreate the cascades and exuberant water displays of the Italian gardens on their rather flat landscape, they were highly influenced by Italian design and imitated many of its details. What evolved in the French gardens of the 17th and 18th centuries was a kind of grandiose Italian garden with the addition of large canals and moats, used for their reflective beauty, surrounding the château. Rustic grottos were often installed, which were directly influenced by Italian examples; some were subterranean pools embellished by famous potters such as Palissy, who is known to have covered much of the surface of one grotto with ceramic tile and sculpted fish, reptiles, and coral in rich colors.

The gardens of the palace of Saint-Germain-en-Laye were quite similar in plan to those of the Villa d'Este, and, in fact, two Italian waterworks engineers, the Francicini brothers, collaborated on the design of the fountains and reflecting basins. They were responsible for a fantastic shellwork grotto that contained figures of a woman playing a water organ, Mercury playing a trumpet, a dragon that flapped its wings, and singing birds. The water displays in French palace gardens were generally dependent upon pumps to raise water from rivers to reservoirs located at a level higher than the gardens to be served. Lead pipes then conveyed the water from the reservoir to the garden.

2-49. Pumping machine at Marly.

There were hand-worked pumps and horse-driven pumps, but the largest and most common were water- and wind-driven, such as the pumping machine constructed at Marly to conduct water to Versailles.

Nicolas Fouquet hired the great garden designer André Le Notre to design the gardens of Vaux-le-Vicomte and received from him such an impressive layout, replete with parterres, water cascades and jets, stately vistas, and statuary, that King Louis XIV, enraged that one of his ministers would live in greater splendor than he, decided to build the greatest palace in all Europe at Versailles. Employing Le Notre, the King spared no expense to create his gardens. Fourteen hundred jets were installed for the fountains, but, even with the advice of the best hydraulic engineers in France, the problem of obtaining enough water for all of them was never resolved. The great pumping machine on the Seine at Marly, described earlier, took seven years to complete but still failed to adequately supply all the fountains. Other attempts had been made earlier to provide sufficient water, such as with horse-driven pumps, a system of draining the surrounding water table into a series of reservoirs, and an aqueduct from the Eure River, which was abandoned before it was completed. There were elaborate water theaters at Versailles, as in many of the French château gardens, which were used as backdrops for festivals, plays, and social gatherings. Although they were shown in great detail in engravings of the period, none of the water theaters has survived intact.

The Italian and French baroque water gardens became popular throughout Europe through publications and through the travels of statesmen, aristocrats, and students of the arts. Germany, Austria, Spain, England, and Russia began to demonstrate this influence by building their own mini-Versailles. Even in the United States many wealthy families built large pseudo-French or -Italian estates complete with water gardens, from the Biltmore estate in North Carolina, designed by Frederick Law Olmsted, to the Hearst estate on the California coast. These American examples, however, were primarily constructed in the late 1800s and early 1900s, a century after most of the European offshoots appeared. An interesting adaptation of the Italian water cascade was constructed in the 1930s in Meridian Hill Park in Washington, D.C. and is one of the few American examples of this style of design.

2-50, 2-51, and 2-52. Fountains of Versailles. (Photos courtesy H. Roger-Viollet, Paris.)

45

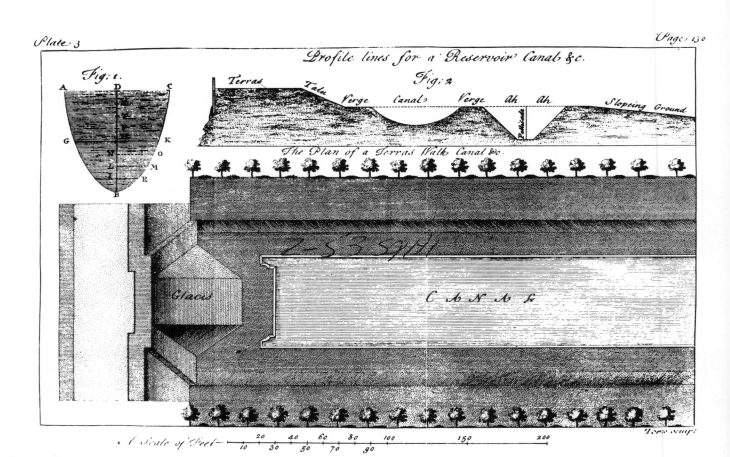

2-53. Standarized canal plan from Stephen Switzer's *An Introduction to a General System of Hydrostaticks and Hydraulics, Philosophical and Practical,* London, 1729.

2-54. Fan jet at Villa d'Este, Tivoli.

2-55. Japanese garden.

CHINA AND JAPAN

The contribution of Chinese and Japanese gardeners to the use of water in design is wholly in the area of natualistic effects. Their method of water design was achieved under entirely different conditions and with a different modus operandi than western gardens. Western gardens and their water features have almost always been created by a professional designer, hired by a client, who then contracted with a third party to install the design. All western gardens and water features are relatively easy to accurately measure and draw up in elevation and plan, as they are derived from specific units of measurement and geometry. Chinese and Japanese gardens, by contrast, were typically designed by poets, painters, and monks who often installed them as well and may have lived on the premises. It is doubtful that many of these gardens were planned in terms of scaled drawings; it is more likely that paintings and sketches provided the basic ideas and that the final product was the result of considerable experimentation and adjustment. Anyone attempting to design a naturalistic rock garden in the West knows the utter impossibility of putting on a scaled drawing an artistic arrangement of rock when the individual rocks have not yet been seen.

The Chinese may have been responsible for the construction of the first man-made decorative lake in A.D. 607 when a gigantic park extending in circuit over 75 miles was constructed with the labor of a million workers. A chronicler of the time wrote that earth and rock were brought to make hills and that the ground was excavated for the Five Lakes and Four Seas, each of which covered an extensive area. The largest, the

Northern Sea, was over 13 miles in circumference, with three island peaks complete with colored pavilions, terraces, and colonnades. This park was constructed by the Emperor Sui Yang Ti near his capital in the city of Lo-yang. Shortly after this park was visited by a Japanese embassy official, the idea that imperial rule demanded great lake gardens to complement the palaces spread to Japan, and the first Japanese land-scaped lake garden was constructed in front of the imperial palace.

Typical of both Chinese and Japanese lake and pond designs is the sinuous layout, interrupted by strategically placed hills, mounds, rocks, and trees that cannot all be seen or experienced from one single spot. Each part instead unfolds and reveals itself to the stroller in succession, always keeping some aspect of itself unknown. None of these gardens was designed for crowds of people or for vast spectacles and social celebrations, as were the western gardens: they were rather places for solitude and contemplation. On their paths two people would even find it difficult to walk side by side. Poets, painters, hermits, and scholars were all held in high regard in China, and it was quite common for these individuals to seek out some particularly inspiring spot to construct a hut or a study and meditation pavilion.

The art of creating a dry stream bed, while orginating with the Chinese, was carried to perfection by the Japanese. Compositions of carefully chosen rocks, sand, gravel, and raked patterns present an image of fluidity unmatched by any details of a similar scale in western gardens. The Japanese, however, did for-

2-56. Chinese garden bridge.

malize and attach symbols to much of the Chinese material and style of garden making to the extent of deriving names for many particular rock combinations and for at least twelve types of waterfalls—such as water falling to the left, to the right, in many threads, in a series of cascades, and so on. They developed very early a series of manuals that established theories and methods of garden design. One 11th-century manual, the *Sakutei-ki* (Memoranda on Garden Making), recommends the following procedure for constructing a stream. "In making a stream in a garden, place the rocks where the water turns: then it will run smoothly. Where the water curves, it strikes against the outer banks, and so a 'turning stone' should be laid here and there as if forgotten. But if too many stones are placed along the stream, while it may appear natural when you are close by, from a distance it will seem as if they had no purpose. Moreover, an excess of rocks will make the course seem one of stone rather than of water. Thus, the water effect will be spoiled." The principles of waterfall construction, pond and island formation, and many other details of garden construction are also included in this manual.

By the 18th century Chinese gardening reached Europe and affected taste to such a degree that formal gardens were torn up all over England and to a lesser extent in other countries and were replaced with naturalistic designs by the new breed of landscape architects, such as "Capability" Brown and Humphrey Repton. The general philosophy of park design that orginated in this period has continued to this day with minor variations. It should be noted at the same time, however, that styles and influences traveled in both directions: the Chinese, upon learning of the grandeur of 17th-century European gardens, asked two Jesuit missionaries to create a series of gardens featuring foreign waterworks. A labyrinth was created that was surrounded on three sides by rushing water, and the Hall of Peaceful Seas—which could be described as Chinese baroque in style—was constructed complete with ramps, monumental steps with jets in the balustrade, and a water clock with each of the twelve animals of the Chinese annual time cycle of twelve years spewing out water in turn for one hour! Unfortunately, these western gardens did not survive: they were destroyed shortly after the fall of the dynasty that was responsible for them.

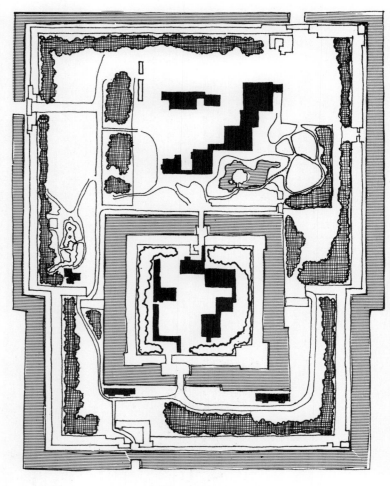

2-57. Plan of Nijo Castle, Japan: informality enclosed within a formalized frame.

3. WATER AS A DESIGN ELEMENT

As we have seen, water has been used as a design element in a multitude of ways throughout the ages, presenting a complexity and interweaving of function, symbolism, and effect that defies simple classification. Only at a fairly gross level can one sort into categories many of the uses of water in design and even then such a classification inadequately describes the full reality and parameters of the areas so defined. At the risk of making such a classification, however, I will briefly describe a few types of water features for each of several environments.

THE SINGLE FOUNTAIN

At the scale of the singular fountain feature one can discern the following general historical types.

(1) *The embellished spring.* Originating primarily with the Greeks, this fountain type served as a source of potable water, which was also endowed with a variety of specific medicinal and legendary attributes.

(2) *The nymphaeum.* An architectural city fountain derived from the previous Greek fountains but more elaborate, including columns and statuary. This type of fountain was highly developed by the Romans and was fairly common even in private villas.

(3) *The fountain of ablution.* Originating in the Islamic world, such a fountain serves as the vehicle for the obligatory cleansing prior to entering a mosque.

(4) *The sculptural fountain.* A fountain type that, originating in the Greek and Roman golden ages, disappeared to some extent until the Renaissance, when it was used as a centerpiece for plazas, courtyards, and intersections. It has become the main prototype of what a fountain should look like and of where it should be located. The majority of factory-made kitsch fountains produced today fall into this category in their attempt to imitate classical quality.

(5) *The imperial fountain.* This is really only a bureaucratic, overscaled version of the preceding fountains, usually the result of a commission by a pope, king, or (in our own age) wealthy benefactor to perpetuate his memory with an overblown, heavy-handed, austere pile of rock or concrete covered with bric-à-brac. Such fountains abound in France, Russia, Germany, and even in some cities in the United States (Buckingham Fountain, Chicago, for example).

COMPOSITIONAL ELEMENTS

Aside from the singular fountain feature, water on a larger, more comprehensive scale has been used in the following ways.

(1) *A frame for a composition.* At Chantilly Le Notre designed a moatlike enclosure that created an effect in which the château floated within a mirrorlike water "frame." A variation is to use water as a setting: water provides the overall setting rather than being merely a feature within it. Large lakes, lagoons, or bays have often been used in this way, with the built three-dimensional forms—land, bridges, shelters—penetrating into the water on peninsulas or islands and providing focal points or activity areas.

(2) *A spine.* Rivers through cities exemplify this expression of water, as do artificial channels, canals, and even some modern street-mall features. Linear in character, water acting as a spine provides both unifying and organizational continuity for an area. If it is developed properly, it leads people to and from particular areas and also serves to separate one element of a design from another. Examples include the beautifully developed urban water channels in Zurich, the old canals of Copenhagen and Amsterdam, the San Antonio riverfront, and portions of the malls in Sacramento and Tucson.

(3) *The heart of a composition.* By being at the center of activity—indeed, by actually creating the center of activity through its presence—water becomes an active and auditory element, creating immediate interest and attracting pedestrians to the source. As a centerpiece this type of water feature should exhibit a sense of scale in relation to its setting and space. This use of water generates attention and activity, may provide a major feature of sculptural art in a public area, and in some ways fulfills the function of an urban oasis. Many such features are to be found in the middle of traffic circles in European cities, where they are unable to fulfill all the functions enumerated in a satisfactory way. A good example of water as the heart of a composition that does fulfill these functions would be the fountain in Ghirardelli Square in San Francisco. Although it is small and unimpressive in comparison to the ornate brick facades on all sides and the views to the Bay, it is constantly surrounded by musicians, tourists, and tired shoppers to whom the sound and sight of water in this small courtyard is irresistibly attractive.

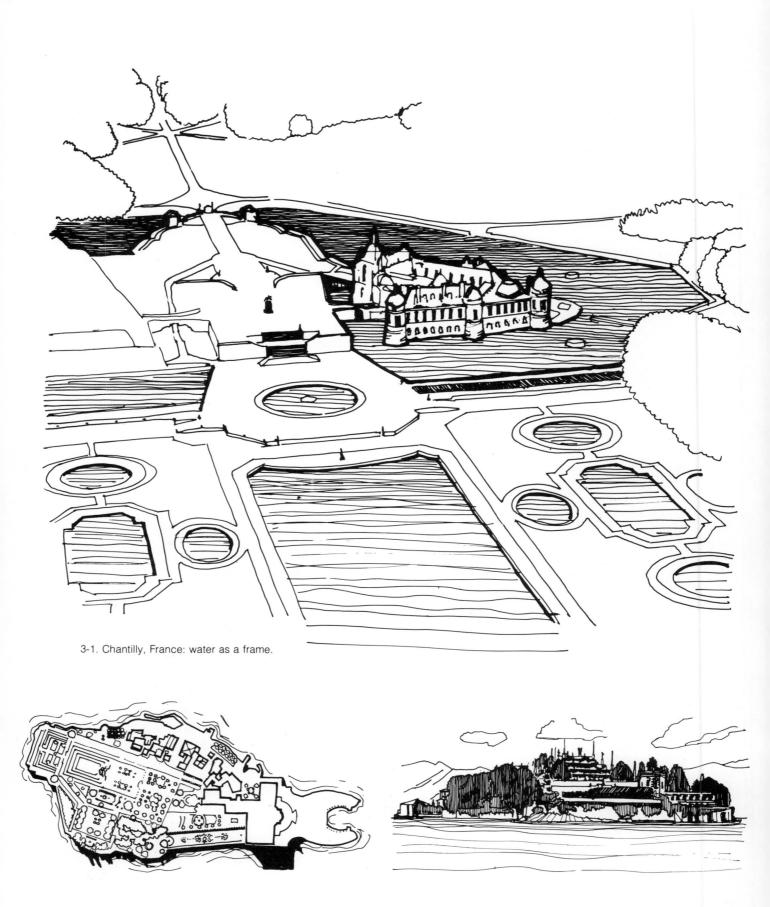

3-1. Chantilly, France: water as a frame.

3-2. Isola Bella, Lago Maggiore, Italy: water as a setting.

3-3. Water as a setting, Denmark, Edith & Ole Norgard, architects.

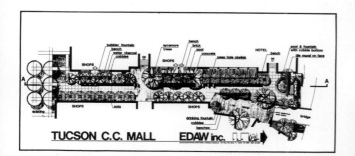

3-6. Water as the heart: University of California at Berkeley.

3-4 and 3-5. Water as a spine: Tucson Mall, by EDAW, Inc.

3-7. Water as the heart: Ghirardelli Square, San Francisco.

LA SALLE DU BAL, est a main gauche entre le parterre des et le Labyrinte, pres la fontaine de Bacchus. Cette piece qui est une des plus belles et riches et destinée pour les Dances, est entourée de deux fossez d'eau, il y a plusieurs Vases de fleurs, et 8. grands Torchetes ou Candelabres pour y mettre des feux la nuit. Les Cascades qui sont au fonds dont la cheute est assez precipitée, font un effet merveilleux a la clarté de ces lumieres la musique se met au dessus et les Spectateurs sur les Sieges de l'Amphitheatre. A Paris Chez I. Mariette rue St. Jacques a la Victoire Avec Privilege.

3-8. The water theater at Versailles.

(4) *A theater or total environment.* While this use of water has a noble and ingenious history, having been developed to its highest level in Renaissance and baroque Italy and France, it is happily enjoying a comeback in a new form. Very few of the older water theaters have survived except in the form of engravings, which give us an idea of the elaborate tableaus that were once commonly staged within them. As settings for social occasions among the aristocracy these water theaters have been minutely detailed in many prints from that era, which show terraced amphitheaters with seats built into semicircular forms, water jets, cascades, parterre water channels, and basins serving as backdrops. That these water theaters were common is shown by the fact that a virtual catalog of such settings, along with various elaborate jets d'eau, was published in the 18th century.

In recent years there have been a number of significant attempts to again create water-enhanced social-recreational settings that can be thought of as giant stage sets. The first was Lawrence Halprin's Auditorium Forecourt Fountain in Portland, one of the most elaborate water features ever constructed in the United States. (I am not forgetting gigantic water displays such as that at the Kansas City Baseball Stadium: they are just not in the same league, if you will excuse the pun.) It is not a coincidence that the project designer of the Portland fountain was formerly a stage designer in Europe. This fountain, more than any other water feature of this century, was responsible for reestablishing the multipurpose, playful use of water as an experiential element, relating it to present-day social and cultural habits and offering an uparalleled space for the widest possible variety of people, moods, and uses. It should be stated here that this fountain was conceived and built before there was much concern about energy or water consumption and conservation, and it is doubtful that another feature would be built on this scale again, at least not without utilizing water that is merely rechanneled from an existing natural continuous flow, such as most of the earlier water features of the Renaissance.

There are several relatively recent water theaters in Europe that are on a monumental scale, but they are primarily used as visual rather than participatory elements. One of these water features is known as the Magic Fountain of Montjuich Park in Barcelona, Spain. A series of huge cascades and jets arranged in a formal manner down a hillside on the grounds of an exhibition site. Another European water theater of recent vintage is located adjacent to the Palazzo dello Sport, a modern sports arena, in a new quarter of Rome. An outdoor amphitheater faces a large display of cascades and jets, which is viewed across a lake.

3-9. Auditorium Forecourt Fountain in Portland, Oregon, Lawrence Halprin & Associates.

3-10. Lovejoy Plaza and Fountain, Portland, Oregon, Lawrence Halprin & Associates.

3-11. Marina Playa apartment complex, California, Brown & Heldt.

(5) *Naturalistic pools, ponds, or lakes.* These features are in a somewhat different category from decorative fountains, and I do not intend to delve into their design and construction very deeply. Such bodies of water vary considerably in their design, due to local climate, soil conditions, size, use, budget, and other mitigating factors. There are commercially available products made primarily from bentonite, an absorptive and colloidal clay, which can be spread over the pervious soil and which will completely seal the surface after it is filled with water. There are methods of layering polyethylene sheeting with clay or sand that perform satisfactorily in small-scale ponds; there are also rubber membranes that are laid down in sheets and even methods of hot-mopping an asphalt surface, which have been used in some decorative

lagoons. All these methods have their own particular uses, depending upon local conditions. If there is any chance of marsh or other gas forming under the waterproof membrane, a plastic-sheet-type treatment will not be sufficient.

To design a seminaturalistic stream channel to carry water through a housing development, the method of constructing the bed partly depends on whether clear water is desired and on the rate at which it will be moving. Gunited concrete with stones embedded in the surface may be used for such a channel in addition to the membranes mentioned. If an opaque or semitransparent quality is desired for the water, little water movement is necessary, and the pond or channel will seem deeper than it really is. With a clay or sand bottom it is very difficult to maintain clear water.

3-12. Footbridge over man-made lake, 6001 Apartments, Redmond, Washington, John Lantzius & Associates.

3-13. De Anza College, Cupertino, California, Royston, Hanamoto, Beck & Aby.

3-14. Granite cobbles used on bank, Syntex Research Center, Palo Alto, California, SWA Group. (Photo by SWA Group.)

3-15. "Wood" posts and "stone" made of concrete with rubber mold forms, experimental shoreline in Alameda, California, Royston, Hanamoto, Beck & Abey. (Genuine wood posts and rock turned out to be less expensive!)

If fish are desired, the water should have a minimum depth of 3' or 4', and it may be desirable to include aeration jets somewhere in the body of water to add oxygen. There are endless possible combinations of naturalistic ponds, channels, hard-edge fountains and pools, jets, cascades, and other features that can be united in many ways to suit a particular environment. The federal government and many state agencies publish pamphlets, primarily directed to farmers, that contain detailed directions for pond construction, including trout ponds.

3-16. Water as a backdrop: Paley Park, New York City.

(6) *Other compositional elements.* In addition to these rather simplistic classifications there are many other ways in which water can be used as a design element. It can be used as a *backdrop,* as in Paley Park in New York City; as an *accent or focal point;* as a *sculptural element;* as a *recreational and visual open space;* as a *utilitarian* potable water source, as in many of the beautiful smaller fountains in Europe and the Middle East; and as a design element that provides a *linkage* between various components of a design, including buildings.

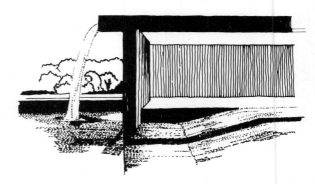

3-17. Water as a symbol: horse-trough fountain in Los Clubes subdivision, by Luis Barragán, Mexico. The fountain is used to water horses.

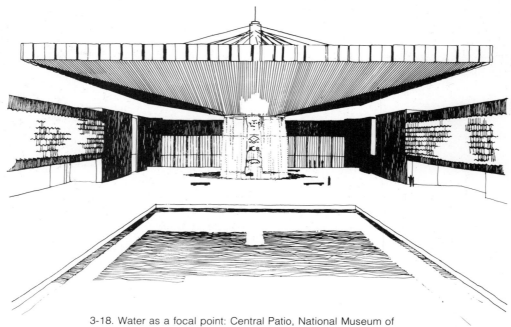

3-18. Water as a focal point: Central Patio, National Museum of Anthropology, Mexico City, Pedro Ramirez Vásquez, architect.

3-19. Water with sculpture: Seattle Playhouse Courtyard. (Bronze sculpture by James Fitzgerald.)

3-21. Sculpture integrated with water in an interior courtyard, San Francisco.

3-20. Water with sculpture: Crown Zellerbach Plaza, San Francisco. (David Tollerton, sculptor.)

3-22. Water and sloping walls used to create an illusion: Medici Fountain, Luxembourg Gardens, Paris.

3-23. Potable water fountain, Zurich, Switzerland.

3-25. Sculptured cast-bronze fountain outlet, Pioneer Square, Seattle, Jones & Jones.

3-24. Glass-roof shelter and drinking fountain, Pioneer Square Seattle, Jones & Jones.

3-26. Water as linkage: The City, Orange, California, Howard S. Thompson & Associates. (Photo courtesy Kim Lighting, Inc.)

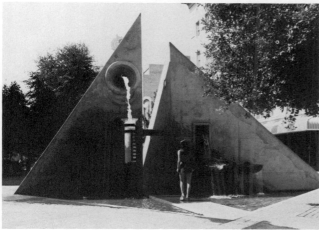

3-27 and 3-28. Playful use of water: Saramento K Street Mall.

3-29. The bathroom fountain in the U.S. Exhibit, Spokane Expo 1974.

In particular situations water may be used in a *humorous* and *playful* way. The Sacramento K Street Mall utilizes water in a great variety of ways throughout its length, but one of the most delightful displays involves water that gushes from a pipe protruding from the face of a triangular concrete form into a giant acrylic test tube, held out as though by a giant steel hand to receive its measure. All the bubbling effervescence inside the tube is clearly visible as the water hits the bottom and makes its way back into the structure from which it emerged. From there it travels over a narrow walkway between the two concrete forms and emerges again into a clear acrylic pipe ell, which again returns its catch into the bowels of the structure only to finally emerge from three troughs. The conceptual design was by EDAW, Inc., and the detail design by Spink Corporation of Sacramento. Another humorous use of water is offered by a fountain in the pedestrian zone of Munich, which presents a playful figure of Bacchus spewing water on a young boy's head. This fountain operates all winter and creates an interesting robe of ice around the sculpture.

3-30. Humorous use of water: fountain in the pedestrian zone, Munich.

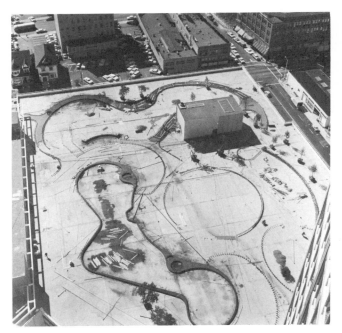

3-31. Kaiser Center Roof Garden (under construction), Oakland, California, Theodore Osmundson & Associates, landscape architects. (Photo by Theodore Osmundson.)

3-32 and 3-33 Kaiser Center Roof Garden pool, Oakland, California, Theodore Osmundson & Associates, landscape architects. (Photo by Theodore Osmundson.)

THE ROOF GARDEN

A number of highly successful water features have been constructed over concrete-slab roof decks. One of the best in the United States is the Kaiser Center roof garden in Oakland, California—designed by Theodore Osmundson & Associates—which features a free-form pool with 8,800 square feet of water surface kept in motion by underwater jets. The pool is 16″ deep and is painted black to give an impression of greater depth. The roof garden was constructed over a 3½-acre garden roof that is highly visible from the Kaiser office tower and other surrounding buildings in downtown Oakland. Another unusual roof garden with water features, designed by Sasaki & Associates for Place Bonaventure in Montreal, is a multipurpose convention center and hotel. High above the city visitors can look out into a lush garden with a naturalistic pool, waterfalls, channels, and boulders—an entirely unexpected experience to those who are unaware of its existence.

There are quite a few types of water features that have been constructed on slabs over parking structures. There is no way, however, to minimize the fact that all construction of this type involves considerably greater costs than the same development would incur if constructed at grade. The structural requirements to support the additional weight of water, copings, sculpture, planting, and other features must be worked out at the preliminary-design stage, and the water features ordinarily have to be designed to fit a particular structural system rather than the reverse. It would also seem that permanent waterproofing is impossible and that all pool bottoms over slabs would probably require periodic maintenance to preserve a watertight condition.

One particular type of water feature that has appeared in a number of locations lately—the *circular waterfall* from a plaza-level pool to a glass-enclosed pool on a lower shop or office level—is questionable due to a number of inherent problems. If the water to be used in the system contains a high quantity of dissolved minerals—particularly calcium—the viewing windows will in short order become coated with a cloudy deposit that is extremely difficult to remove. This particular type of waterfall detail also seems to create more serious leakage problems than are found in water features situated only at the top level of a plaza deck. Every installation of this type that I have encountered has experienced serious problems that continued to plague the consultants involved and the owners long after completion.

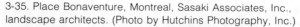

3-35. Place Bonaventure, Montreal, Sasaki Associates, Inc., landscape architects. (Photo by Hutchins Photography, Inc.)

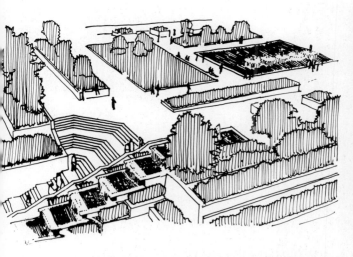

3-34. Mellon Square, Pittsburgh, one of the first garage-roof plazas with water features built in the United States.

3-36. Las Palmas Park, Sunnyvale, California, Ribera & Sue, landscape architects, Taylor & Ng, sculptors. (Photo by Tom Tracy.)

3-37. Serra Park, Sunnyvale, California, Ribera & Sue, landscape architects.

PLAY AREAS

Water features are ideal in play areas, particularly in sections of the country with long, hot summers. If the water features can be controlled or adjusted to some degree by the children, so much the better. The most perfect example of user control probably occurs when children in New York City and other eastern cities open up fire hydrants during heat spells. There are probably more imaginative play areas with water features in California than in the rest of the country combined, partly due to a climate favorable to year-round use but also to the receptivity of public officials and citizens to good design. Many of these play areas involve sculptural forms, water, and landscape unified in such a manner that they are as much works of fine art as they are recreational features.

Water installations in play areas are often designed to flow directly from city water systems, through the apparatus, and into drains without being recirculated, since they are not turned on all the time and usually do not involve great volumes of water. In this manner filtration and chlorination systems may be avoided. Special vandalproof spray heads designed to be installed flush with the pavement are available from some fountain-equipment companies. If water is held in a wading pool, the depth should be very shallow and the bottom should be finished with some sort of texture so that it is not slippery. All spray jets should be designed to deliver water at relatively low pressures in pool areas to prevent eye damage to children who place their faces directly into the stream of water. In the case of large wading pools, of course, filtration and chlorination is necessary if the water is recirculated.

MOTION IN WATER FEATURES

Surge or *wave action* can be created artificially in a confined body of water by making one portion of the side or bottom of the pool movable or by introducing additional water or air pressure at a given point. A number of artificial-wave machines have been constructed, some for recreational use in pools and others—such as the one at the Montreal Expo '67 exhibit—purely for visual enjoyment. Luis Barragán designed a small surge basin in the courtyard of a hotel in Mexico City that mysteriously boils up in an agitated manner every few seconds, an effect every bit as interesting as the more common cascades and jets. The mechanical systems required to properly operate this type of display may, however, be prohibitive. At one major office building in New York the architect is reported to have conceived of a wave of water that

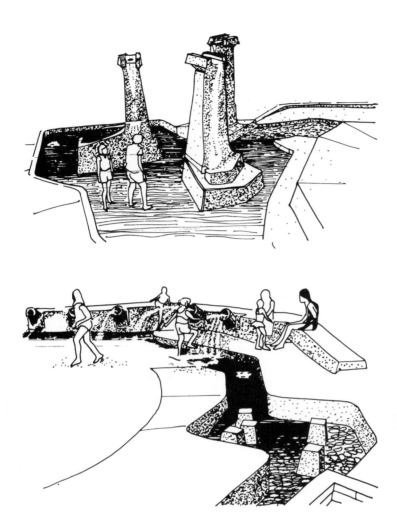

3-38. Portal Park, Cupertino, California, Ribera & Sue, landscape architects.

3-39. Olympia Water Gardens, Olympia, Washington, Lawrence Halprin & Associates.

would surge from one end of a long pool to the other, but, when it was determined that it would require a 36″ discharge pipe and a 400 h.p. pump, the idea was dropped in favor of conventional spray jets, which were not too successful.

Another seldom seen type of water display is the *kinetic-sculpture fountain,* in which water is used to turn or move various objects. While these displays can be a lot of fun and can offer a humorous contrast to the more serious displays, they are often short-lived, as they are exceptionally prone to vandalism or breakdown. They are usually more suited to temporary exhibits or installations in highly controlled surroundings. An exception is the sprinkler-head assemblage designed by Jacques Overhoff, which was built at the Seattle World's Fair site in 1962 and is still functioning in a perfectly riotous manner. On the other hand, several less durable kinetic-water-sculpture installations involving moving wheels, cups, and fins that were in-

stalled at shopping centers in Detroit and Indianapolis are now inoperative.

One of the best kinetic-sculpture fountains in recent years, designed by the Russian-born sculptor Naum Gabo, was installed recently at St. Thomas Hospital on the south bank of the Thames opposite the House of Parliament in London. The entire work, which is 9′ high, revolves slowly on its base, making one complete turn every 10 minutes. The water effects are varied by increases and decreases in the water pressure at regular intervals. Gabo was one of the first sculptors to experiment with kinetic sculpture, and his treatment of water in this work produces a striking interplay with the metal forms from which it emerges.

While they are often discussed at a preliminary stage of design, the idea of *people-operated water features* is rarely brought into reality. There are, of course, practical considerations of economics and vandalism that can never be ignored, but there are

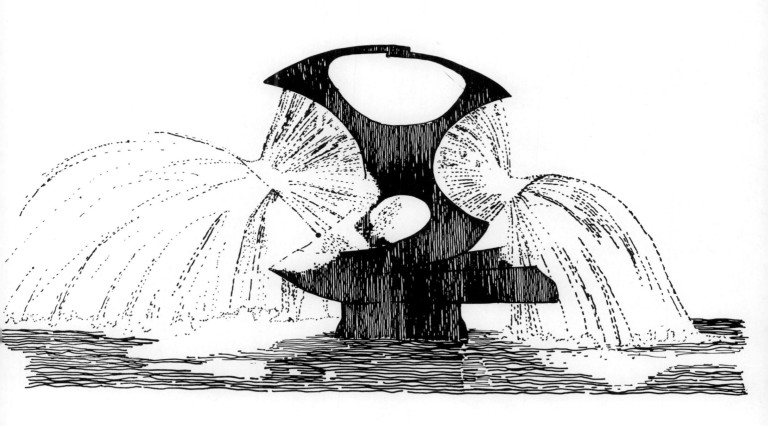

3-40. Kinetic Sculpture Fountain by Naum Gabo, London, England.

relatively simple ways to allow people to control water flow that have been included in some fountain designs. In children's play areas, of course, spray jets are available that are operated by means of a solenoid valve activated by a time-delay pushbutton switch. When a child pushes the button, the spray comes on for several minutes, avoiding continuous operation and consequent waste. The switches are similar to those used in pedestrian crosswalks.

A very successful sculptural fountain was installed in front of the new Seattle Water Department Operations Center building, which features two large people-operated wheel valves controlling the flow of water. This fountain was the result of a statewide competition held by the Seattle Art Commission to choose a design that would reflect the basic nature and purpose of the Water Department: "Since the work will become a major source of identification for their Operations Control Center, the Water Department recom-

mends a work involving a great quantity of water—one which uses water as the primary sculptural element, rather than other structural materials. The forceful and effective use of water exhibited by each proposal will be of primary importance to the jury. The value of involvement by an engineer familiar with hydraulics should not be underestimated, and the technical feasibility and reliability of the proposal will be a prerequisite." The sculptor who submitted the winning entry, Ted Jonsson, proposed a design using two huge polished stainless-steel pipes in a sculptural form that would be extended by the water. The resulting project involved the Water Department, the architects (Burke Associates), the engineers (Ben Notkin & Associates), and the sculptor. Half-size prototypes were tested at the University of Washington Hydraulics Laboratory, and a full-size model of the pipe orifice was constructed to test the concept of mounting smaller nozzles inside the stainless-steel pipe around the opening

3-41. Seattle Water Department Operations Center Fountain. (Photo by Ray Welch.)

to provide the illusion of a solid column of water. The completed project is a delight to behold, particularly in the semiindustrial setting in which it is located, and is a tribute to the vision of Kenneth Lowthian, Superintendent of Water, who originally initiated the project by allocating a portion of his budget to art. The completed project fulfills many of the functions that I have mentioned: it provides an appropriate *symbol* of identification for the Seattle Water Department; it offers a *focal point;* it represents an excellent work of modern *sculpture;* and, finally, it offers the opportunity for *audience participation.*

UTILITARIAN WATER FEATURES

When enough pressures are brought to bear on officials responsible for certain projects that are usually thought to possess only a utilitarian function, such as dams or fish ladders, it is sometimes possible to expand the project, exploiting water as a recreational and educational tool while still fulfilling the original function. One recent example is a fish-ladder structure proposed for Grand Rapids by the Michigan State Department of Natural Resources to assist salmon and steelhead in getting upstream to spawn. Joseph Kinnebrew, a sculptor, managed to convince the local politicians and business leaders that the fish ladder offered a superb opportunity to combine sculpture, architecture, and public involvement in a structure that also serves the function of aiding the fish in their movements. Kinnebrew, in consultation with the architectural firm of Wold, Bowers, DeShane & Covert, produced an exceptional solution that serves as a means of environmental education, in contrast to the proposed purchase of a large work of sculpture by an international figure, which was supported by many city leaders.

A similar structure, built on the Capilano River in North Vancouver, British Columbia, also provides an opportunity to actually watch fish as they travel from level to level and to learn through outstanding interpretive displays about the biological environment and life cycles of salmon. Many other opportunities are available in a myriad of forms if imaginative people will only look into the possibilities for enlarging and enriching the roles of otherwise single-function projects.

3-42. Sculptural Fish Ladder, Grand Rapids, Michigan.

4. PRINCIPLES OF DESIGN

HYDRAULICS

As mentioned in the first chapter, the art of fountain design flourished and became more intricate as *hydraulics*—the practical applications of water in motion—evolved in the 16th to 18th centuries. It must be understood, however, that, with most large water features, there are no exact formulas for predicting the action of water unconfined in pipes and that engineers and designers in past centuries undoubtedly faced the same uncertainties and trial-and-error situations encountered today in fountain design. Since the velocities, pressures, and flow patterns associated with complex, irregularly shaped water features can only be approximated by mathematical calculations, a simplified version of the true flow pattern is ordinarily adopted as a working guide. For this reason the construction of working scale models of complex fountains is a prerequisite in many situations of the working drawings.

The mechanics of stationary fluids—*hydrostatics*—has been understood in some detail since Archimedes' remarkable two-volume work on the subject appeared about 250 B.C. One of his more important discoveries, known as *Archimedes' principle,* states that the buoyant force on an immersed body is equal to the weight of the fluid that it displaces. Leonardo da Vinci, through his notes and sketches dealing with falling jets, surface waves, flow in pipes and through orifices, and hydraulic machinery, contributed further to the development of hydraulic principles. Leonardo

expressed what is now known in a more refined form as the *continuity equation.* He noted that the velocity of a river is linked to its cross-sectional area: in a river of constant depth a reduction in width produces a corresponding increase in speed. The Dutch mathematician Simon Stevin published a significant work on hydrostatics in 1586 and demonstrated that the total force on the base of a vessel is equal to the weight of the column of fluid above that surface even if the sides are irregular or sloped. The Italian physicist and mathematician Evangelista Torricelli contributed an important principle of hydraulics in the early 17th century when he discovered that the speed at which a liquid flows out of a hole in the side of a tank is equal to the speed attained by a drop of liquid falling freely from the level of the upper surface of the liquid to the orifice. The French scientist-philosopher Blaise Pascal essentially completed the theory of hydrostatics in 1650. *Pascal's law* states that pressure in liquid is transmitted equally in all directions, a principle that served as the basis for the development of the hydraulic press.

In the early part of the 18th century the rise of classical *hydrodynamics* (the study of fluids in motion) coincided with the contributions of two important pioneers in the field, Daniel Bernoulli and Leonhard Euler. Bernoulli showed that the pressure exerted by a moving fluid decreases as the fluid speeds up and increases as the fluid slows down. The *Bernoulli equation* is an energy-conservation equation that indicates that the total energy in 1 pound of liquid remains constant as it

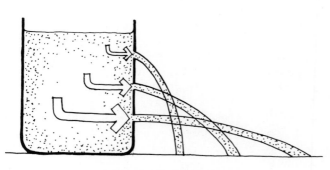

4-1. Torricelli's Principle.

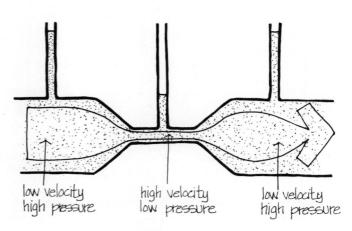

low velocity high pressure   high velocity low pressure   low velocity high pressure

4-2. Bernoulli's Principle.

flows, regardless of changes in velocity, height, and pressure, from point to point along its path. The refinement of this equation, which allows it to accurately take into account changes in pressure and density, was made possible by the contributions of Euler, a brilliant Swiss mathematician. In the late 18th and early 19th centuries more basic work was done in the area of theoretical hydrodynamics, and the formula for predicting the velocity of flow in channels was developed by Antoine de Chézy. Increasingly refined studies undertaken on various aspects of fluid flow, viscosity, pipe resistance, vortex motion, and other specific topics ultimately led to the more general science of *fluid mechanics,* which is applicable to both liquids and gases.

There are quite a number of good volumes available on the subject of hydraulics, and it is not my intention to offer more than a brief summary of the development of hydraulic principles and a simplified description of what they represent. All major fountain designs require mechanical, electrical, and structural consultants, the earlier in the project, the better. The architect or landscape architect responsible for the conceptual design of a water feature should have at least some awareness of hydraulic principles, as they often affect the feasibility of particular design concepts.

Two distinct states of motion are encountered with fluid flow.

(1) *Laminar flow.* In this state water or another fluid moves in a smooth, straight, parallel path at a rate less than 1½″ per second through a 1″ pipe at atmospheric temperature.

(2) *Turbulent flow.* In this state water or another fluid moves at a rate over 2½″ per second through a 1″ pipe at atmospheric temperature, resulting in a turbulent, fluctuating, whirling movement that causes an agitated mixing of the fluid. If the temperature, the liquid, or the size or shape of the conduit changes, the speed at which laminar flow changes to turbulent flow will also change. The concept of laminar versus turbulent flow is central to fountain design, as only a laminar-flow condition will produce certain waterfall and jet effects. Both velocity and depth of the basin often have to be adjusted to alter flow conditions from turbulent to laminar.

Another characteristic of fluid motion is the clinging of fluid elements to boundary walls, forming a retarded flow layer. Fluid mechanics has thus influenced the shape of boats, for example, to minimize the disparity of front and back pressures of the water by attempting to create a symmetry of flow patterns with a minimum of drag force. In fountain design this condition is met by notching or otherwise designing spill lips so that the water falls free rather than clinging and running along the underside.

While it is possible to predict with reasonable accuracy the velocity and pressure distributions of given flows through pipes—which are primarily laminar-flow motions—it is much more difficult to predict the effects of turbulent flow if the effects of viscosity are complex. *Viscosity* is the state or quality of fluids that modifies flow patterns according to a particular formula, based on V (velocity), D (width of the obstacle of flow passage), and v (value of viscosity). In the formula $R = VD/v$ the Reynolds number, R, represents a value for which the smaller the number, the greater the modifying effect of viscosity on the flow pattern. If the value of R for flow in a pipe is greater than 2,000, the flow will be turbulent; if it is less than 2,000, it will be laminar.

As mentioned previously, the multitude of parameters within which a given water-feature system is moving can present some difficult problems for a hydraulic-engineering analysis. Most formulas are straightforward in terms of water in pipes, but in terms of systems of cascades, open channels, obstacles, and textures, which may present conditions as varied and complex as a mountain stream, they are not too helpful. In order to arrive at answers regarding predicted flow rates, required pump sizes, and other criteria, the standard calculations are inadequate and must be supplemented by a laboratory scale model, which offers a more accurate and visible picture of the flow characteristics of water in a proposed design.

The flow pattern ideally should be a steady one: that is, one in which the flow rate does not vary appreciably from time to time. (If an automatic valve quickly closes and retards the flow, allowance may have to be made for the increased pressure effects of the compressing water column.) If water flows uniformly between parallel walls or in a straight pipe, the mean velocity is the same at any cross-section point. If the boundaries are not parallel or if flow is toward a waterfall or sink, the flow is nonuniform and does not follow predictable models.

The basic concepts of hydraulics have not changed appreciably for over a century. The three basic equations are the continuity equation, Bernoulli's equation, and the momentum equation.

The *continuity equation* deals with the fact that the velocity of a fluid increases as the area of the flow path decreases: in other words, a given volume of water moving through a 10″ pipe increases in velocity if the pipe size is decreased, say, to 8″. If the cross-sectional area is halved, the speed is doubled. As the velocity increases, the pressure on the pipe walls decreases. The basic understanding of this principle is ancient, and nozzle and inlet design from Moorish Spain, for example, indicate the use of widening or narrowing openings to increase or decrease pressure and velocity.

Bernoulli's equation links the various forms of energy (described below) in a formula that can be used to predict one form of energy or the flow of water at a given point if the other factors are known.

The momentum equation states that the rate of change in momentum of a fluid is directly proportional to the applied force. Both the Bernoulli and the momentum equations are derived from Newton's second law of motion, which applies equally to solid bodies and to fluids.

The *energy* of water represents the capacity of water to do work and can be calculated if the velocity, pressure, and height above a certain level are known. Each of these characteristics gives water the capacity to do work: the velocity gives it kinetic energy; the pressure, pressure-different energy; and the height, elevation or potential energy. One type of energy can be transformed to another type. The measure of the energy of 1 pound of water is the height in feet to which it can raise a weight of 1 pound of anything, including itself.

Given a jet of water with a speed V at ground level, the jet should rise to a height given by the kinetic-energy equation: $h = V^2/2g$. V is the speed in feet per second, and g is gravitational acceleration, 32′ per second. As all energy in this case is kinetic, each pound has sufficient energy to raise 1 pound (itself) to a height of $V^2/2g$ before coming to rest and then falling back.

In a tank of water maintained under a pressure of p pounds per square foot water is allowed to escape through an orifice in the top, creating a jet that issues vertically. This jet will rise to the height in feet given by the *pressure-energy* equation: $h = p/w$, where w is the weight of water per cubic foot (62.4 pounds). The pressure energy of water is p/w: each pound of water is able to raise 1 pound (itself) to this height due to its pressure above atmospheric.

Elevation energy or potential represents the simple ability of a descending pound of water to raise an equivalent weight into the air to the same height, h, as the original height of the water.

The *total energy,* E, of 1 pound of water flowing at a speed V, under pressure p, in a pipe h feet above the ground would be the sum of its kinetic, pressure, and elevation energies: $E = V^2/2g + p/w + h$ energy units. The total energy of water as it passes through pipes or over hills remains unchanged and is the basis for Bernoulli's equation, which allows for the calculation of an unknown element if the other factors are known. By using a venturi meter, which measures the pressure drop at a constriction in the pipe, the rate of flow of the water can be calculated with the continuity and Bernoulli equations.

Several commonly held beliefs about the nature of water are not true, at least not in all circumstances. One is the notion that water always seeks its own level and that it cannot run uphill. If it is enclosed in a pipe, of course, it does flow uphill as long as the outlet is lower than the source; most water systems involve considerable uphill flow within the overall network. Wave action on a beach also makes water flow uphill, as do certain obstructions or bottom configurations in a stream. Another fallacious notion is that water is incompressible. In fact, it is slightly compressible, and pipes would burst in valves closed under pressure if water were absolutely incompressible.

When water drains from a container, the normal movement is counterclockwise in the northern hemisphere and clockwise in the southern hemisphere. What is not so widely known is that spiral movement also takes place on a horizontal plane in river channels, and this characteristic motion, exhibited in the pattern of wear and deposit in the stream bed, is the cause of the serpentine course of rivers flowing through broad, flat areas.

DESIGN CONSTRAINTS

Anyone who has studied the history of fountains in the United States or around the world is aware of the rather cyclic fashion in which they seem to occur and then recede in various cultures. Around the turn of the century fountains proliferated in American cities, partly as a result of the City Beautiful movement stimulated by the Chicago World's Exposition in 1893. Only a few decades later many were shut down and dismantled, a victim of the economies forced on the country by World War I and the depression. A number of massive water features built in the 1960s in various cities are similarly either in partial operation or transformed into planting beds. This latter type of recycling is a sore point, especially when it happens even to a fountain as carefully thought-out and planned as one in San Francisco that was written up in architectural journals because of the scale-model testing of prototype design features in the University of California hydraulics laboratory. This fountain involved a magnificent but simple use of water flowing in a thin sheet over the edge of a 34-square-foot slab of granite with no jets or fancy effects of any kind, yet this fountain has been turned into a flower bed!

Situations such as this point up the importance of achieving a complete understanding with the client regarding the required maintenance program and costs. Too many fountains have similarly been lost due to designs that were too costly for owners to maintain properly. It should be understood, however, that questions of size, cost, and complexity of water features are as much related to prevailing cultural and social values as to conservation issues and economics. For example, a large water feature affords a multitude of delights to thousands of people and is often partly responsible for rejuvenating the life and soul of a downtown area. If these effects are given high values in the minds of officials and the public in a particular city, then ways will be found to build and operate such features. There is a rationale for luxuries when they serve a multitude of purposes at one time and when they are afforded to the many rather than the few. Many students of the urban scene have noted that in America private amenities have always been assigned a higher priority than public amenities and that in European cities the opposite has generally been true. That situation thankfully seems to be slowly changing, and many American cities, such as Portland, Minne-apolis, Boston, and Seattle, now offer more genuine urban delights in their central areas than a good many of their European counterparts.

Having offered the argument in favor of major public water features in our cities, it should also be stated that a great deal more can be done with quite small volumes of water than is generally realized: fountains don't have to be on the Portland scale to generate excitement and activity. There should also be more attempts in the future to utilize water from existing rivers, streams, lakes, and rainfall-runoff structures, re-channeling it and borrowing its energy in imaginative ways, as did the Italian and Moorish designers in the past. Installations are now being planned to utilize solar pumps and mountain-stream water for a large display in Vail, Colorado, and New Mexico ranchers have been experimenting with similar pumps for irrigation purposes to replace pumps run by natural gas, which have become uneconomical to operate. With the increasing problems posed by water shortages and the need for energy conservation, it is doubtful that we will see many more water features in this country on the scale of some of the larger ones illustrated in this book. Since a goodly number of the larger projects were financed in the past with generous urban-renewal funds, we are likely to see more conservative uses of water in the future, consistent with the financing and maintenance abilities of city governments and private foundations. Many of the larger water features that were originally developed by urban-redevelopment agencies with federal funds were transferred after completion to city administrations already strapped for maintenance funds, and in many cases, after tallying their fountain maintenance and operating costs for the first year, these cities discovered that there was no way in which they could afford to operate the water features at the capacity for which they were designed. Water, of course, is generally recirculated, but more must continually be added to compensate for evaporation. Furthermore, all fountains must be completely drained and cleaned out periodically each year. And there is no way to ignore the energy costs required to operate a 350 h.p. pump, for example, or the maintenance costs for all the other complicated appurtenances of a large fountain.

The Embarcadero fountain in San Francisco, which was the result of an international design competition, illustrates these problems. The gutsy concrete forms—which to some observers resemble the

4-3. Embarcadero Fountain, San Francisco.

dynamiting of the elevated-freeway structure in the background—were designed to spew out a volume of water consistent with the large, square openings of the concrete forms; due to operating economies only a fraction of that amount flows out, totally out of proportion to the size of the sculptural elements. The sculptor's concept also called for the viewers to experience a foglike atmosphere as they walked around and through the water feature, which entailed installing a boiler and steam pipes under the fountain with outlets hidden under the overhang. To my knowledge this expensive feature was operated only once, on opening day—which is the best example I know of the importance of achieving a complete understanding with the client or agency that will inherit the fountain and be responsible for its maintenance.

At the earliest possible stage both the designer and the client should discuss all the ramifications of installing a fountain that will offer as few problems as possible and be maintained as required to keep it operating efficiently. Poor locations, adverse microclimatic conditions, low budgets, and many other factors may rule against *any* water feature whatsoever, and these factors should be faced squarely. It is a shortsighted mistake for any designer to ignore some of these problems in attempting to persuade a client to go along with a water feature that will ultimately be a monument only to the folly of the architect. If there is not complete accord between owner and designer regarding both construction costs and realistic operating costs, the designer may win his way but will not benefit in the end.

On large projects maintenance people assigned to the water features will ideally have some background in plumbing-system maintenance rather than strictly garden or building maintenance. The maintenance supervisor may be included in some of the mechanical discussions at the design stage and should be provided with a complete set of drawings and a mintenance-program handbook upon completion of the project. In this manner any questions regarding the maintenance program can be discussed at the proper stage. To merely be handed the drawings upon completion of the project is tantamount to being given the manual for orbital docking maneuvers!

Basic Considerations

The following are important considerations that should be examined in the early stages of a proposed fountain design.

(1) *Location.* Dusty, windy locations pose almost insurmountable problems for all water features, as water is a superb air filter and returns to the basin or pond everything that it has pulled from the air. It is difficult to keep strainers and jets from clogging up in such locations, and pool floors will rapidly gather debris and have to be drained and cleaned frequently, boosting maintenance costs to a high level. A windy situation can be managed in the design, although the options for various water effects are quite limited. If wind is a problem only part of the time, a wind-control device can be installed that automatically reduces jet heights or stops them altogether when the wind exceeds a set velocity.

(2) *Purpose.* Is the fountain to be located in a public pedestrian area? Are there likely to be many children in the area? Is the water feature to be a main attraction or merely an architectural linkage element in the landscape? Virtually all large water basins must be treated as swimming pools with filtration and chlorination systems. Signs prohibiting entry are fine, but they don't stop anyone who really wants to get wet!

(3) *Maintenance.* Who will be responsible for overseeing the operation of the fountain? If it is a janitorial staff, it is wise to avoid complicated systems that may require frequent adjustment and attention. For a fountain of large size and complexity, it is preferable to appoint a person who will have the water feature as one of his prime responsibilities and who will understand in some detail the mechanical system that operates it.

(4) *Feasibility.* After eliminating egotistical considerations and combining common sense with the available budget and the above factors, does it still make sense to build a fountain? If so, continue!

Fountain Checklist

The following questions represent a composite list of factors to be considered by fountain designers at both beginning and advanced stages. It is partially drawn from lists published by various fountain-equipment companies.

(1) What purposes will the fountain serve—entertainment, symbol, focal point?

(2) What are the local conditions affecting the fountain or being affected by it?

(3) Will the fountain be accessible as a wading pool?

(4) In plan are there isolated pool areas that are difficult to circulate?

(5) Is the pool suitable for winterizing without removing equipment?

(6) If multilevel cascade pools are involved, is the lowest pool large enough to contain the circulating volume (volume of water in transit) of all the pools above it?

(7) Is the suction-screen area large enough based on flow requirements? The free area of screen should have no less than an 8:1 ratio to inlet piping, and there should be a maximum design velocity of 1' per second at the suction inlet.

(8) Is the pump selection adequate not to overload the pump(s)?

(9) If water-level-dependent jets are used, are water-level controls provided?

(10) If vertical jets are used, are swivel unions or adjustable nozzles used?

(11) For winterizing pools with pits are double-drainage systems used? Is the pipe system designed for complete draining?

(12) Are pump chambers and mechanical room well ventilated? Can they be gravity-drained or must a sump pump be installed?

(13) Are all electrical conduits in water made of red brass, and is the electrical plan in accordance with article 680 of the National Electric Code?

(14) In windy areas is a wind-control device included? If it may be necessary at a later date, are provisions made for it?

Potential Problem Areas

Outlined below are some problems to look out for.

(1) *Large-area shallow pools.* These pools are difficult to filter properly, unlike swimming pools with a sharp slope, which forces debris to one area. Shallow pools also promote the growth of algae, which require chemicals to control. With continual water movement, of course, these problems can be overcome, but in a still or barely moving pool they have to be contended with.

(2) *Small-orifice jets.* Even with the best filtering system these jets will often clog up and have to be removed and cleaned. The larger the openings, the better.

(3) *Automatic valves.* While these valves are a must in complex systems that must be independently operated for changing effects, most of them have tiny ports with minute openings, which, like small-orifice jets, can easily become clogged even with a good filter system. In many of the newer automatic valves, however, these small ports have been eliminated, lessening the problem of clogging.

(4) *Splash.* Underestimating the splash problem is one of the most common errors in fountain design and can be serious enough to warrant closing down a fountain entirely. Although there can be no set formula, due to wide variations in design specifics and local conditions, the width of the basin should generally be at least double that of the height of the jets or even four times the height in a windy area. On certain types of pavement, such as terazzo or even smooth concrete, water can create such a slippery condition that owners have been held liable for accidents. The United States is unfortunately one of the most lawsuit-prone countries in the world: in most European countries liability insurance of the type expected of most cities and companies here is unheard of. Unlike swimming-pool perimeters, the pavement adjacent to pools should be sloped toward the fountain to avoid uncontrolled run-off if there is any likelihood of splash. If there is a raised coping, however, this will not be possible without a perimeter drain.

(5) *Hard-water supply.* In some parts of the country in which municipalities draw their water from wells the amount of calcium and other dissolved minerals is considerable and can clog fine orifices in nozzles or control valves. As water is added to a pool to compensate for loss through evaporation, the hardness of the pool water increases beyond that of the supply water. If the water is extremely hard, a commercial water softener may have to be introduced into the system. Pools in such areas will have to be drained and the water changed more frequently than usual, probably at least once every three to four weeks, depending upon local conditions. All spray from hard-water fountains should be kept away from windows to avoid mineral deposits on glass.

(6) *Vandalism and debris.* Although there is no such thing as a vandalproof water installation, certain types of design and specific fittings offer the least possibilities for vandalism. If a pool is located in an area with a lot of loose rock, bark, or other debris, you can expect some of this material to end up in the fountain. No filtering system will remove large or heavy objects or coins from a pool: they must be cleaned out by hand. Undersizing the recirculating-system suction-screen area is one of the major errors encountered in fountain design and can lead to rapid clogging of the intake by debris and closure of the pump, which can do irrevocable damage.

Quite a number of fountains installed around the country in recent years feature jets of some sort that do not fall into a standing pool of water: water is instead either immediately drained into the recirculation system at the base or carried in a thin sheet over a sloped surface to a drain. The maintenance problems and potential for vandalism are greatly decreased if there is no standing water. Some of these fountains offer the option of closing the drains and temporarily allowing a basin of water to collect, which is the sort of flexibility to be desired in water features. One such fountain, the Copley Square Fountain in Boston, designed by Sasaki Associates, Inc., features a very impressive sculptural raised basin from which rise a number of large aerated jets into the air; the water falls along the grooved, sloping sides of a truncated pyramid base and is immediately drained into a sump for recirculation without being allowed to gather in a pool except if desired.

As I have already stated, today's water features, if they involve water maintained in basins as contrasted with fountains of the type just described, must generally be treated as swimming pools in both design and maintenance program. The historic water features of Moorish Spain, Persia, Renaissance Italy, and many other past cultures involved borrowing moving water from springs and streams; rechanneling it into reser-

4-4. Copley Square, Boston, Sasaki & Associates, Inc., landscape architects.

4-7. Fountain at Westbeth Artists Community, New York City, Richard Meyer & Associates. (Photo courtesy Kim Lighting, Inc.)

4-5 and 4-6. Copley Square Fountain, Boston.

4-8. Fountain, St. Louis, Missouri, Peckham-Guyton, Inc., architects. (Photo courtesy Kim Lighting, Inc.)

voirs, aqueducts, channels, or pools; and returning it to irrigation ditches, lakes, or rivers, with the water usually in continuous motion. We, on the other hand, usually deal with closed systems that pose many problems of contamination as well as necessitating more elaborate systems of plumbing and artificial circulation. Another obvious detrimental factor is the lack of large crews of permanent maintenance personnel and gardeners, associated with all the great water features of the past.

Virtually every major new fountain is a prototype, with no comparable model against which to judge performance, costs, or maintenance problems. This fact also gives water features their special distinction, as they are so utterly unlike buildings or even normal plumbing or mechanical systems. Each has to fit a new set of conditions; no two are ever exactly alike; and each must be treated with cautious respect, knowing that it probably will not do exactly what you expect it to do. For this reason it is always a good idea, whenever possible, to construct a scale-model mock-up of the proposed design, which can then be fitted to a flow of water of proportionately the same volume. Although the effects are not precisely the same as in a full-size fountain, a scale model allows both architect and mechanical consultant to most closely approximate the real situation, even with simulated wind conditions, and to make adjustments as necessary to refine the design at an early stage.

Ice and Fountains

The effects created by allowing fountains to operate in winter, building up ice mounds of ever-changing sizes and shapes, can be truly magical and should be considered in colder climates whenever feasible.

The Kansas City Parks and Recreation Department has been experimenting with winter operation of fountains for a number of years and has found that very little damage is caused by the ice. Most problems were due to the weight of the ice mass and affected the supports of the fountain equipment. Spray nozzles were sometimes bent, but the effects of the ice varied from year to year, depending upon changes in wind, thaws, amount of sun, and other factors. Having learned through experience to anticipate problem areas, Kansas City now allows a number of selected fountains to operate all year, providing a new source of enjoyment in the winter. The fountain basins can often be used for skating, and the ice mounds as a playground and climbing area irresistible to children.

By carefully designing fountains at the beginning to withstand the weight of ice and keeping exposed plumbing systems to a minimum, it should be possible to extend use throughout the year even in the coldest climates, although at a somewhat reduced level of water circulation.

DESIGN CONSIDERATIONS
Scale

Byron McCulley of Lawrence Halprin & Associates correctly points out the primary importance of *scale* to fountain design. He emphasizes the "size and volume of the fountain or pool relative to the overall spatial environment in which it will be located. This means examining the situation in as large a context as appropriate, not just within the immediate surroundings. It also means looking at the *volume* of space in which the element will be located—height, width, depth. If buildings are adjacent, the scale of the individual buildings must be considered as well as their scale as a complex."

The relative size of the various components in the water display is also important, as is the relationship between the water area in a fountain and the hard components. The most satisfactory method of determining proper scale relationships, both of fountain to surroundings and of individual components of the fountain itself, is by constructing a scale model that can be adjusted and altered until the best solution is found.

4-10. Scale-model mock-up of proposed fountain in Munich, Germany, designed by Prof. Bernhard Winkler. (Photo by Bernhard Winkler.)

4-9. Ice mounds, Three Fountaiins Apartments, Albuquerque, New Mexico. (Photo © Ray Cary, *Albuquerque Journal.*)

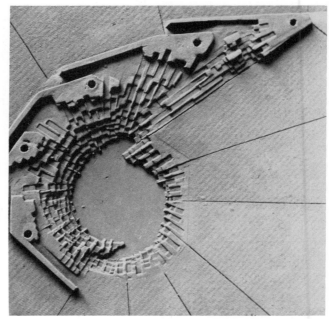

4-11. *La Barcaccia* (The Old Boat) fountain in the Piazza di Spagna, Rome.

Immediacy

Architect Charles Moore has given considerable thought to the many aspects of water and emphasizes the need for *immediacy,* or the closest possible contact between the observer and the water. Both psychological closeness as well as actual contact with the water are required: he offers as examples the fountains of Rome, which often step down below the level of traffic, forming rims to sit on that often dip down under the surface of the water. Some of the recent American and European fountains go even further in providing a multitude of possibilities for contact with water. If any single design consideration stands out above all others, it is precisely this sense of immediacy, the opportunity for direct contact with water and the fewest barriers.

4-12. Natural basalt-rock columns used in water channel, Spokane World's Fair, 1974.

4-14. Marble fountain, Puebla, Mexico.

4-13. Granite-block fountain at the Frauenkirche, Munich, Germany, designed by Prof. Bernhard Winkler. (Photo by Bernhard Winkler.)

4-15. Black-granite fountain, Federal Reserve Plaza, Minneapolis.

Sunlight

An often overlooked factor in designing water features is an orientation that takes advantage of direct *sunlight:* it is usually not taken into account until the fountain is already built. All jets and waterfalls are spectacularly transformed when they are viewed with the sun behind them, illuminating the spray and every crystal drop of water. Site constraints sometimes work against exploiting sunlight to advantage, but, whenever possible, the effects of direct sunlight on water should not be overlooked. Even some otherwise mundane water features become very attractive when the sun is at the proper angle.

Materials

While almost all early pools and fountains—for example, in Moorish Spain or Renaissance Italy—were made of *stone,* sometimes combined in Italy with bronze statuary, this material is only rarely used in fountain and pool construction today due to its high cost. When it is used, black or red *granite* is the most common choice for several reasons. The first is that it is available in large, monolithic units that can be cut to exact final shape by stonemasons (usually employed to carve tombstones) near the quarry. Secondly, wet granite exhibits its superb grain and coloration far better than most building stones. Several impressive foun-

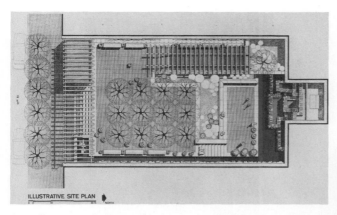

4-16. Greenacre Park, New York City, Sasaki & Associates, landscape architects. (Photo courtesy Sasaki Associates, Inc.)

4-17. Greenacre Park with night lighting. (Photo courtesy Sasaki & Associates.)

4-18 and 4-19. Greenacre Park waterfall.

tains installed in the last 10 years in the United States utilize granite for the entire water display. The most elaborate is Greenacre Park, funded by the Rockefeller Fund, which is a delightful little oasis tucked between two buildings in Manhattan. Designed by Sasaki Associates, the park features an impressive 25' waterfall that cascades over sculpturally composed granite blocks set at the far end of the three-level space. Granite is also used in combination with Corten steel in an overhead trellis and shelter on the west side and in a sculptural block wall designed to "weep" water over the rock to a channel below. This park is owned and maintained by a foundation set up for that purpose—the Greenacre Foundation. It is open seven days a week, and attendants are on duty at all times. This type of administrative organization is ideal in certain areas when an elaborate water feature is involved, as the opportunities for vandalism are greatly decreased if an attendant is visibly keeping an eye on things. Granite has also been used in fountains in which the entire pool basin—up to 30' in diameter—is carved of one block of stone. If the budget allows for its use, granite is certainly an incomparable material for water-feature design and construction.

4-20. Vail, Colorado, Royston, Hanamoto, Beck & Abey, landscape architects. (Photo by Royston, Hanamoto, Beck & Abey.)

Boulders and *rock* are often used in seminaturalistic pools and fountains. The natural rock is sometimes used both as the container and as the central sculptural element in a pool, with jets of water or waterfalls emerging from the rocks and falling into the surrounding pool. The firm of Royston, Hanamoto, Beck, & Abey was responsible for a large plaza design in Vail, Colorado featuring a naturalistic water display that utilizes 300 tons of native granite boulders to create a series of multilevel cobble pools and cascades.

Brick provides an exceptionally rich texture on pool surfaces. It is almost always utilized as a veneer over concrete, however, and must be used with a certain degree of caution. Brick varies considerably in its absorption capacity, depending upon the particular clay used, the density, and the firing. All brick used underwater must be treated with a clear, waterproof sealant: even brickwork adjacent to water areas should be sealed. The quality of the joints is of prime importance in fountain construction with brick.

4-21. Napa Mall fountain, California, Sasaki & Associates, Inc., landscape architects.

4-22. Mears Park, St. Paul, Minnesota. (Photo by William Sanders.)

4-23. Brick fountain in Seattle, Richard Carrothers, landscape architect.

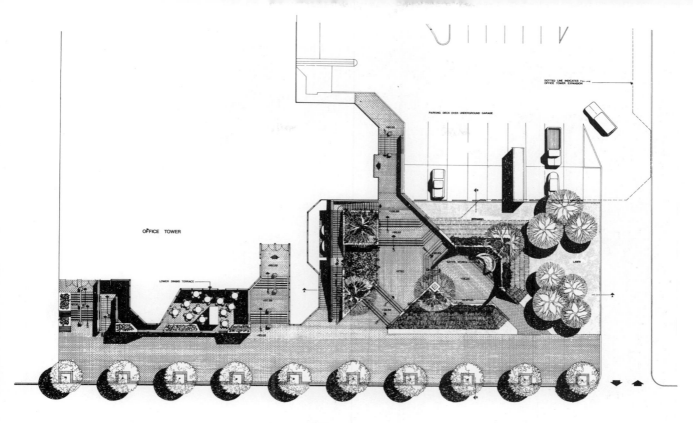

4-24. Century Bank Plaza plan, Fong & LaRocca Associates, landscape architects. (Photo by Fong & LaRocca.)

4-25. Century Bank Plaza fountain, Los Angeles. (Photo by Fong & LaRocca Associates.)

4-26. Wilshire Pocket Park, Los Angeles, Fong & Associates; landscape architects. (Photo by Julius Shulman.)

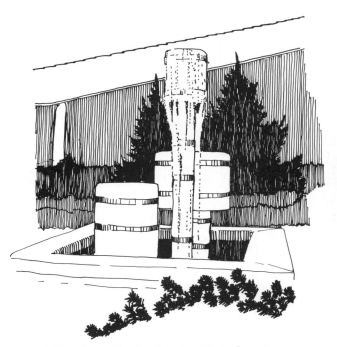

4-27. Driftwood-log fountain, Sun River, Oregon.

4-28. Civic Center Plaza Fountain, Albuquerque, New Mexico, Flatow, Moore, Bryan, & Fairburn, Inc., architects.

Metal is rarely used except in small pools and in sculptural elements. Both copper and sheet brass have been used for small pool basins, and both ultimately achieve an attractive coloration with contact with the water. In larger pools with chlorination systems, however, these same metals will turn black. Sheet lead was once a very common pool liner, especially in conjunction with ceramic tile facings, but this material is now usually utilized only if a pool is placed over an occupied space in a multistory building in order to ensure a completely watertight basin.

Fiberglass offers the advantage of light weight, although it is not particularly durable. It does have its place if weight is a factor, in temporary installations, and in small pools where cost is a factor. A number of companies offer complete fountain "kits," which include predrilled fiberglass basins, submergible pumps, jets, and all fittings and probably account for more installations than all other types of fountains combined.

Even *wood* has been used successfully in fountain design. Some of the sculptural play units manufactured by Timberform in Oregon are combined into a very interesting wood fountain in a park in Portland, and another, constructed of large driftwood trunks, spouts water in front of the lodge at Sun River in Oregon.

Concrete is the most common material used in pool construction for the same reasons that it is the most common material used in major building construction and in highway bridges. Concrete can be formed into almost any shape; it is readily available; workmen experienced in handling it abound; it is relatively inexpensive; it is durable; and it can be colored and finished in a wide variety of ways. Unfinished concrete, however, does not enhance the quality of water and therefore should receive some sort of texture and color surface treatment. Integral colors can be added to concrete to give it the quality of stone and to provide a warmer tone. The colors most often used range between the tans and ochers to brick red or red-brown. In some cases, particularly to reflect an adjacent material or a stone sculptural feature, concrete should be colored black, but this has disadvantages, which are detailed in the section on pool bottoms later in this chapter. Other methods of enhancing the surface of concrete are: texturing obtained with special formwork such as boards with exposed grain; creating relief patterns, which offers an endless number of possibilities; tooling the surface with a bush hammer or by sandblasting it; top-seeding river-washed aggregate into the surface; and applying finishes or veneers such as mosaic tile. The major problem with concrete is probably its susceptibility to surface cracks. If the concrete has been properly mixed, poured, and cured, however, this problem should not arise. If a concrete pool is found to have a leak after completion, it can be plugged with materials that expand on contact with water.

Precast concrete is an excellent material that is

4-30. Fountain of precast-concrete elements, De Anza College, Cupertino, California, Royston, Hanamoto, Beck & Abey, landscape architects.

4-29. Concrete fountain in private garden, Germany, Hans Luz, landscape architect.

4-31. Precast-concrete basin, De Anza College, California.

commonly used for precisely detailed fountain basins or for other components that have a particularly refined design or function. Precast concrete may be very intricately detailed and finished, as it is accomplished off the site under controlled conditions, and it produces a superior product. Precast components are often combined with poured-in-place concrete in a single water display. One company, Western Art Stone, located in the San Francisco area, produces numerous beautifully formed concrete fountain components with surfaces as finely finished as cut stone. Joints between the precast components and the poured-in-place portions of a pool or fountain must be very carefully designed and installed to prevent the possiblity of leakage.

4-32, 4-33, 4-34, and 4-35. Gunited fountain, Park Central Plaza, Denver, Colorado, Lawrence Halprin & Associates, landscape architects.

4-36. Gunited water channel with cobbles and boulders, Marina Cove, California, Singer & Hodges, landscape architects.

Although they are more commonly used in swimming-pool construction than in decorative fountain installation, *gunite* and *plaster* are excellent materials that offer great flexibility of form. Because gunite can be sprayed to a thin depth over a lightweight frame or armature, it is a good material to consider if weight is a factor, as over roof decks. One of the reasons why gunite is not more widely used may be the fear that an inexperienced contractor may do a poor job. At the same time lack of experience on the part of designers may also play a part. The best use of gunite in fountain construction that I have seen is a rather elaborate, seminaturalistic sculptural assemblage of tapered blocks, complete with waterfalls and cascades, that Lawrence Halprin & Associates designed for an office plaza in Denver, Colorado. It is such an exemplary design that it is rather surprising that it is not shown more frequently in the design journals. This project was apparently the forerunner of the larger-scale Lovejoy Fountain in Portland, designed by the same firm. Gunite can also be economically and successfully used to form the bed of naturalistic streams designed, for example, to wander through housing complexes. Boulders are often hand-set along the perimeter of the stream bed, and river rock can be set like cobbles into the bed before it completely sets. This type of water feature is quite common in apartment developments in California.

4-38. Sculptural pool bottom forming islands, Seattle Center, Everett Du Pen, sculptor.

Fountain Features

Reflectiveness can be one of the main features of a pool if it is located in the right setting. Water can be made to appear dark, deep, and thereby more reflective by using a black or dark-colored finish on the bottom and sides of the pool. A black finish, however, will cause the water to absorb more heat than a light-colored one and thus will promote the growth of algae more readily, particularly in a shallow pool. Dirt and debris will be less visible on a dark-colored bottom than on a light-colored one. The dark-colored finishes cause the surface of the water to act mainly as a mirror of external surfaces, which is desirable in some cases but not in others. With a light-colored surface the water appears clear and sparkling, and the bottom of the pool becomes a major part of the design that should not be underestimated.

4-37. Mosaic-tile mural on pool bottom, Standard Oil Plaza, San Francisco, Theodore Osmundson & Associates, landscape architects, Alphonso Pardenas, mosaic-mural designer. (Photo by Theodore Osmundson.)

Pool *bottoms* can be treated in a sculptural way, rising out of the water as free-form islands here and there; they can also be treated as underwater murals, with carefully designed patterns of mosaic tile, larger glazed ceramic tile, or naturally colored cobblestones. The smaller the unit of decoration, the more fluid the movement generally seems to be, as the ripples of water refract the light in differing ways. Small tiles, in other words, seem to have more motion than larger tiles as a person looks down into the water. River-washed cobblestones can be very effective: they offer a natural richness that suggests the feeling of the riverbed from which they originated.

The depth of a pool usually ranges from 8″ to 24″, with greater depths sometimes required in upper basins. If underwater lights are to be placed on the pool bottom and not cast in place, the depth must be a minimum of 10″ to allow clearance with sufficient water over the lights. By keeping the depth under 18″ or 24″ (depending upon the locality) a pool is not classified as a swimming pool under local codes and is thus not subject to the rigid design requirements for that type of classification. The shallower the basin, the less total volume of water must be replaced when the pools are drained and cleaned.

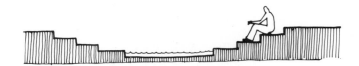

4-39. Stepped-down and stepped-up fountain basins.

4-41. Brimful basin at Las Arboledas, Mexico, Luis Barragán.

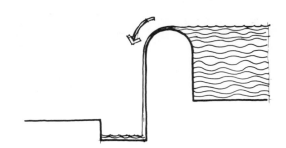

4-42. Rounded rollover-type rim with catchment channel.

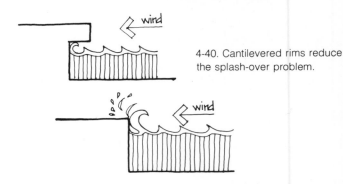

4-40. Cantilevered rims reduce the splash-over problem.

Edges, copings, channels, and *weirs* are important components of fountain design that can be handled in a wide variety of ways. An elevated rim that can also be used for sitting seems to be the most common edge for containing water, although some of the most dramatic and successful water displays have no rims. Care must be taken in designing a pool with no raised rim to ensure that the pedestrian is made aware, through an obvious change in paving texture or through other means, that he or she is approaching something significant. The ground or paving surrounding the pool can be sloped away from the pool edge to prevent debris from washing into the water, but, as mentioned previously, the paving must be sloped toward the pool if there is a likelihood of splash-over from jets. With either slant there will be more problem with wind-blown debris than in pools with raised copings. Pools are sometimes located at the bottom of a stepped-down circle or square, with the stepped levels used for seating. Exactly the opposite arrange-

ment, steps up to a pool, has also been used successfully, as, for example, in the plaza pool in Ghirardelli Square in San Francisco. Pool rims should preferably be detailed with a slight cantilever over the water in order to create a shadow line that will hide the stain area caused by fluctuating water levels. This overhang should be used whether or not the rim is flat or raised. The cantilevered coping is also very important to keep water in the pool under heavy wind conditions or if the display itself generates waves.

In most Moorish basins or pools the water is kept brimful or overflowing at all times, which can essentially eliminate the appearance or at least the dominance of the rim in a design. Luis Barragan of Mexico City designed an extremely long raised-trough reflecting pool slightly overflowing with water all around, which terminated at a dramatic high wall in the middle of a grove of large eucalyptus trees. The reflective qualities and impact of this pool are truly dramatic, particularly in the setting within which it is situated.

4-43. Rounded rim, L'Enfant Plaza, Washington, D.C., I.M. Pei & Associates, architects. (Photo courtesy Kim Lighting, Inc.)

4-44. Rounded-granite-rim detail, Christian Science Headquarters, Boston.

4-45. Intricately sculpted rim of cast bronze, Ruth Asawa, sculptor.

Rims used in this way should ideally be as narrow as possible at the surface. An illusion can be created of a suspended, unconfined sheet of water, a very effective device in the right surroundings. Rounded rims often give this appearance and offer an interesting effect as the water rolls over them.

4-46. Embedded rocks used to create turbulence, Lake Forest, El Toro, California, Courtland Paul, Arthur Beggs & Associates. (Photo courtesy Kim Lighting, Inc.)

In designing channels as part of a water display it is possible to greatly increase the visibility and sound of a given volume of water by introducing obstructions or steps into the channel. If turbulence and white water are created, a relatively small volume of water can be made to appear much greater and to possess a much more forceful and dramatic presence. This principle has been utilized for centuries: the Islamic gardens of Persia and northern India frequently include sloped cascades with built-in zigzag ridges, called *chadars,* to produce a white-water effect. Many of the staircase cascades of Italy and Spain also utilize means of increasing turbulence.

Weirs and spill lips must be designed to relate to the volume of the *waterfall* in motion over them. If small quantities of water are flowing over spill lips, the spill edge may have to be constructed of metal to provide an absolutely level surface and designed to project

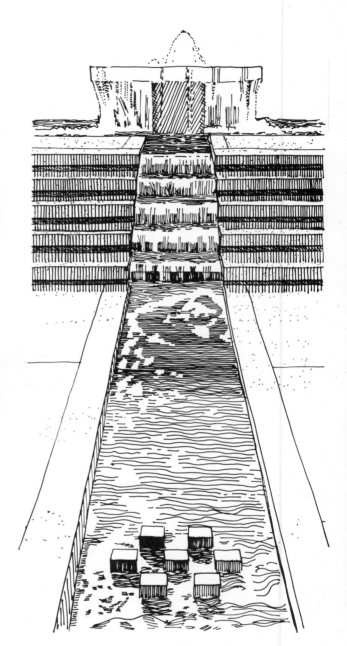

4-47. Blocks in channel used to disturb the surface of flowing water, private residence in Hillsborough, California, Lawrence Halprin & Associates.

out from the face of the adjacent vertical surface. In this manner water is directed outward in a smooth sheet even at low flow rates and does not cling to the face of the wall. The underside of this lip should be notched, however, regardless of the material, in order to break the surface tension and to prevent some of

4-48. A strictly utilitarian dam in Wichita, Kansas provides an exuberant display of water. (Photo by Tessendorf, the *Wichita Eagle*.)

4-49. Metal spill lip, Sacramento Mall.

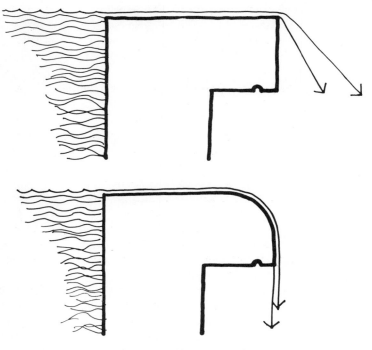

4-50. Square and rounded spill lips.

4-51. Fluted spill lips, Berger Fountain, Minneapolis, Robert Woodward.

the water from clinging and dripping from the under-surface instead of dropping free. A wide variety of effects other than that of the flat sheet may be obtained through the design of the spill lip or edge. An irregular or jagged surface will produce a fragmented sheet; fluted, drilled, or notched edges will break the falling water into separate streams that offer a rhythmic pattern of light and dark, with the light reflecting off the individual streams quite dramatically. When the velocity of water flowing over a weir or lip reaches a certain point, the water will not fall vertically but will instead fall at an angle, increasing with the velocity, away from the face. This is especially true if the lip or weir edge is square; if the upper surface is rounded off, the water tends to drop somewhat more vertically regardless of velocity. If a completely closed curtain of water is involved—such as a continuous-sheet waterfall from a round or square raised basin—there are special problems involving differential air pressures and the venturi effect that prevent the water from dropping cleanly and vertically into the pool. In such unusual cases a mechanical engineer may find ways to offset the pressure differential. In one such installation in California a professor from South Africa was called in by the mechanical consultants to solve this problem.

4-52. High-velocity water falling at an angle over a square edge.

In designing waterfalls the splash problem should not be underestimated in determining the size of the pool at the base. While specific conditions such as wind, water volume and velocity, and other variables play a part in the final design dimensions, a general rule of thumb is to allow a horizontal pool distance equal to two-thirds the height of the falls. The volume of water necessary to achieve the desired effect in a waterfall must be very carefully considered at an early stage, as it is related to the required design depth of the basin behind the falls, to the width of the lip or weir, and to the detail design of the spill lip.

Thin-sheet waterfalls are very effective, but if the flow of water allows a thickness of only, say, ¼" at the lip and if the construction is concrete, there may be a problem in sustaining a flow over all sections of a wide lip. Even the best concrete contractors cannot pour to a tolerance of much more than ¹/₁₆", and, if there is more error in a portion of the lip, the flow may be broken. There are two ways to avoid the problem: (1) to fabricate the lip from metal or precast it in concrete off-site to an exact tolerance and (2), which is preferable, to increase the depth of flow at the lip. As a general guide a ¼"-thick flow at the lip will amount to approximately 10 gallons per minute for each lineal foot of lip. A thickness of 1" will give you about 30 gallons per minute per foot of lip. Some of the more impressive fountains featuring waterfalls have a depth of water at the lip up to 3", involving tremendous volumes of water. Another method used to obtain an absolutely level flow lip in concrete is to form a slightly raised triangular strip along the lip, which can then be ground back as necessary after water is placed in the pool.

One of the most important considerations in the design of *multilevel waterfalls* is the need to provide sufficient depth to reduce the supply-water velocity enough to level the surface into a laminar-flow condition. Overlooking this problem is a very common error in design, and the result is turbulent flow that does not have time to level out before flowing erratically over the edge. A common illustration of this effect is to try to fill a 5-gallon bucket with a fire hose: the velocity it too great for the bucket to fill up to the brim. The same situation may be encountered in providing supply water to a raised basin that will overflow into a lower one: the velocity must somehow be reduced by delivering through multiple outlets, or the size of the basin increased. A system of baffles is sometimes introduced at the supply outlet to decrease turbulence and velocity. Baffles may also be placed slightly behind the spill-lip area in the form of perforated brass sheets below water level to level out the flowing water and eliminate tidal-wave effects. The velocity of water introduced into these pools should generally be no greater than 3' or 4' per second. If the pool is long and rectangular, the supply water may be introduced at several different points in a long trough.

In any system of multilevel cascade pools it is *very* important to size the lowest basin to allow sufficient freeboard depth between the operating level and the top of the coping, since the water will rise in the lowest basin when the pumps are shut off as the volume in circulation settles into the lowest pool. The depth to which the water will rise will be in relation to the volume in circulation. Unless there is sufficient freeboard, the overflow, which should be set at the static water level,

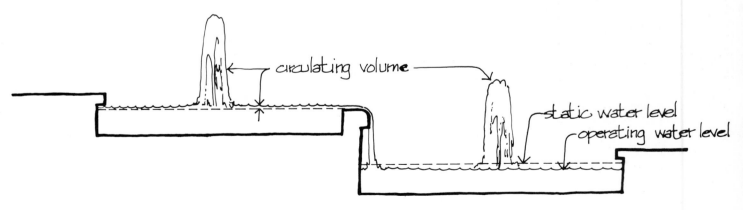

4-53. The lowest basin must be properly sized to accept the operating volume if pumps are shut off.

may be too low (if mounted in the sidewalls) and the circulating volume will go into the drain whenever the pumps are shut off, necessitating replenishment of that volume between each pump operation.

If waterfalls are directed in front of cavities, the sound will be magnified and carried forward much more than with a flat surface. Renaissance and baroque fountains often exploited this principle in an awesome manner if we are to believe the accounts of the incredible echoes, moanings, and roars that they created with such cavities and falling water. Another principle is that, the shallower the receiving pool, the higher in pitch the sound of the water will be as it splashes, as there is less depth to absorb or cushion the falling water.

Another effect not to be underestimated is to allow for pedestrians to walk behind the cascade or waterfall and look through it. The great Ovato fountain at the Villa d'Este offers this opportunity to visitors, and it remains to this day an intriguing and irresistible experience.

In visiting the Moorish gardens of Spain one discovers a wealth of delightful old bronze nozzles that are pieces of sculpture in themselves. Many of them feature decorative valve systems attached to the base of the nozzle, and no two seem to be exactly alike. It would be interesting if some of the fountain companies in the United States sponsored a competition for the design of some new sculptural nozzles: it might help us to get away from jets that resemble miniature cannons and toilet-tank fittings! Although *jets d'eau,* as they are referred to in all old texts, whether French or English, have a noble and lengthy history, they are the source of most of the problems in water displays. One man who makes his living by manufacturing and selling jets and other fountain components confided to me that he would not be unhappy if no fountains were built with jets, as he greatly preferred sculptural water features from both an aesthetic and a maintenance standpoint! Jets do have their place, however, and are often combined quite well with sculptural water features. The truly incredible variety of jets on the market today offers the creative designer an infinite range of possibilities for different sounds and patterns, and, when combined judiciously with an interesting overall concept, they can fill out and complete a design.

In the absence of wind conditions water shooting vertically from a smooth-bore jet will encounter water falling back after reaching its peak and therefore will fluctuate in height as it alternately pushes this water out of the way and is then lowered by it again. Many jets now come equipped with adjustable joints that allow for precision alignment after installation. It is sometimes best to adjust such jets to an alignment slightly off vertical to allow the water to fall to one side. On the other hand, the fluctuation height and action of a jet may often be part of the attraction. If a single-jet nozzle is designed to deliver a stream of water 30′ or more, vane-straightening devices are often built into the jet to prevent the water from leaving the orifice in a spiral movement that would affect the vertical accuracy.

4-54. Bronze jets from Moorish gardens in Spain.

4-55. Moorish jet in the Alhambra: could it have inspired the Coke-bottle design?

There are four major types of jets: aerated jets, spray heads, smooth-bore nozzles, and formed nozzles.

Aerated jets introduce air into the discharged water in order to create a full and foamy effect, with high light-reflection characteristics. Most operate on the venturi principle, which draws air to an area of lower pressure. All aerated jets were originally designed to be discharged underwater so that the jet itself would not be visible. While they were quite popular with designers, these jets—which are still sold—pose a number of problems. The most important is that they require more pressure to reach the same height (having to first push water out of the way) than a jet mounted above water, increasing the required pump size to a significant degree if many of them are utilized. *Water-level-independent* aeration jets are now available that create essentially the same effect of pulling air into the water and may be mounted above the water surface.

Three different types of aerated jets are commercially available. *Bubbler jets* create a low mound (up to 18″) of aerated water that offers bulk and apparent mass with relatively little water and is especially useful in smaller pools or locations with a wind or splash problem. They must be mounted below water level, with the air intake extending above surface. *Foam nozzles* are water-level-independent aeration jets that also utilize the venturi principle but are constructed with a double sleeve that allows air to be pulled into the water even though it is mounted above water level, demanding lower water pressures. *Geyser* (or *cascade) nozzles* are designed so that the nozzle opening is below water with a collar extending around and above it to prevent uneven pouring of water into the area over the nozzle; the area beneath the collar just over the opening is open and allows some of the pool water to be carried up with the cascade jet water, causing a tearing action that produces a heavy column of water.

As much of the water delivered up into the air from an underwater nozzle is out of control, the splash problem is often greater than with a smooth-bore jet. Bubbler-type jets in particular can be quite uneven in their delivery height if used in a small pool, as water becomes shallow and then deeper over the nozzle, but this is also one of their more interesting characteristics.

Aeration jets are often mounted in a cluster on a

4-56. Bubbler jets. (Photo by PEM Fountains, Richmond Hill, Ontario, Canada.)

common delivery-distribution box, which can produce a spectacular effect with relatively little water. All jets are capable of considerable variation in height and general effect, depending upon the volume of water (in gallons per minute) that is forced through the jet. Some fountain-equipment manufacturers provide charts in their catalog that give the precise height that each of their jets will reach under different volumes.

If you are using jets that must be mounted just below the surface of the water, there is little tolerance for fluctuations in water level: water must be kept about ½″ above the nozzle. This calls for very sophisticated water-level monitoring and makeup systems. These jets can also cause a tidal surge within a basin, which has the effect of covering and then uncovering the nozzles. If this condition occurs, the nozzle will alternately shoot water up to the normal height when it is covered with water and suddenly shoot up two or three times the normal height when it is uncovered, as it does not have to push through any water. The basins therefore have to be large enough to avoid surge with aerating nozzles of this type. In certain circumstances perforated baffles extending to just under the water surface are placed on the floor of the pool. There are generally fewer problems and lower water-pressure requirements with aerating jets that are water-level-independent or that work equally well mounted below or above the water surface.

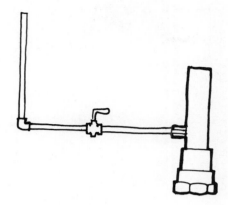

4-57. Bubbler jet.

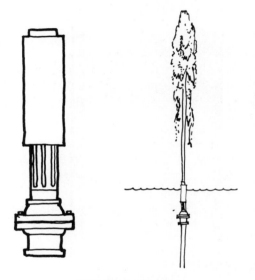

4-58. Foam nozzle.

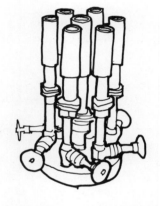

4-60. Aeration-jet cluster.

4-61. Spray head.

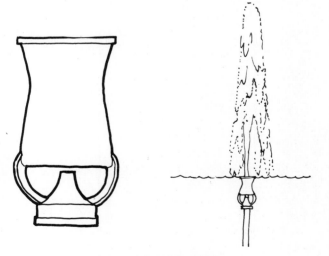

4-59. Geyser (cascade) nozzle.

Spray heads come in an endless assortment of shapes and types and ordinarily consist of a number of fine jets mounted in some sort of pattern on a single distribution head, often in a circle or a fan shape. The circular heads sometimes have holes drilled through the top plate rather than exposed nozzles protruding from it, and, although the uniformity of each water spray will not be as true as with a tubular nozzle, they are more vandalproof and are often used in children's play-area spray pools.

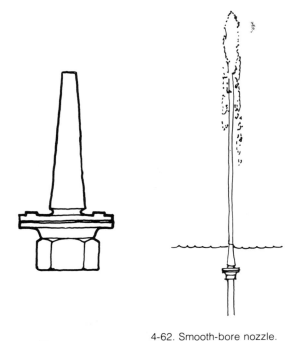

4-62. Smooth-bore nozzle.

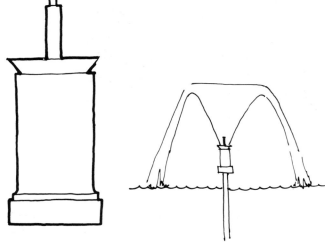

4-63. Formed nozzle, calyx and mushroom shapes.

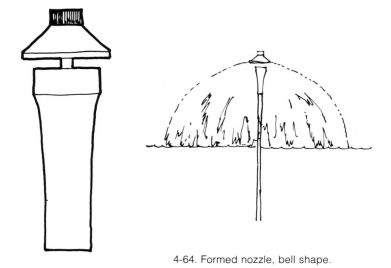

4-64. Formed nozzle, bell shape.

4-65. Formed nozzle, fan shape.

Smooth-bore nozzles are the simplest of the larger jets, consisting of cast bronze with a smooth-bored single channel that, like almost all jets, decreases in diameter toward the opening in order to increase the velocity of the water. These nozzles come in a wide range of sizes to allow almost any height of jet desired. Although this type of nozzle involves the least water breakup and therefore more control, attempting to shoot a fine stream too high can break the water up into fine droplets. These heads are often provided with integral ball swivels that allow an adjustment up to 15° for precise alignment. They are also used in circles or lines by mounting a series of jets on a single pipe manifold. It is sometimes difficult to balance these systems so that all jets are the same height, as the pressure at each jet varies somewhat.

Formed nozzles are shaped in order to produce a certain pattern, and the range of possibilities seems to be infinite. Some of these heads are adjustable and may be set to produce a flattened morning-glory shape or an almost vertical cone. As these heads usually utilize a thin sheet of water for their effects, tolerances are very exacting and the results can be affected adversely by dirt in the nozzle, wind, and other factors. The so-called dandelion fountains are made up of many formed nozzles on the ends of pipes attached to a spherical distribution chamber.

These water spheres or hemispheres are now offered as standard items by most fountain companies, a situation that has unfortunately made them somewhat of a cliché. The patterns are formed by directing water into a hollow distribution ball drilled to receive a series of small tubes, each of which is capped with a machined flat spray head that creates a fine circular pattern of water. The spheres come as large as 16′ in diameter—which is the size of the sphere at the Berger Fountain in Loring Park, Minneapolis (designed by

4-66. Dandelion sphere, Berger fountain, Minneapolis.

Robert Woodward of Sydney, Australia). Because the water spray from these spheres is so fine, considerable mist is created, which must be taken into account in any design. A second problem is potential clogging of the numerous fine orifices, which, even if only a few are clogged, is very noticeable.

Using decorative pools to double as basins for air-conditioning water is perfectly feasible under certain circumstances and should be attempted more often than it is. Using sprays to cool water through evaporation has long been practiced, and there is no reason not to design pools and sprays that can function both as decorative elements in the landscape and as part of the heat-exchange system of a building. The Christian Science Headquarters complex in Boston features a very large reflecting pool that also serves as a cooling pond, and there are others on a smaller scale around the country.

One of the most intriguing fountains that I have ever seen is the lawn-sprinkler fountain located in a naturalistic pool at the foot of the Space Needle at the Seattle Center, which was constructed for the Seattle World's Fair. Consisting of dozens of standard lawn-sprinkler heads, impulse heads, rotating arms, and other devices, all connected to an open-framework structure made up of the water-distributing pipes themselves, it is a glorious, ever-changing effusion of mist, spray, and rainbows that never fails to engage the attention of all passers-by. It was designed by sculptor Jacques Overhoff of San Francisco and Lawrence Halprin & Associates.

It has been stated that a successful fountain depends upon both thoughtfulness and thoroughness throughout the entire process of design, construction, operation, and maintenance. In designing a fountain the basic concept must be related to the mechanical realities as soon as possible in the design process. The concepts of size, location, positioning of elements, and general effects, which are usually the first ingredients of a preliminary design, must be related to the functional requirements and realities by involving the mechanical and electrical consultants in the basic design process at an early stage. Several firms of mechanical and electrical consultants on the West Coast have developed a specialty in the field of fountain design as a result of a close collaboration with landscape architects and architects on the design of some very successful water features.

5. DESIGN PROCEDURES

The prime design procedure to be followed is to *establish the flow rates* necessary to achieve the desired objectives. The desired appearance may be simply a certain number of jets shooting to a certain height, or it may involve more subjective qualities relating to the character of the water in cascades or waterfalls. In dealing with complex water features in the latter category it may be necessary, as mentioned previously, to build a mock-up, or scale model, which can be used to help determine both effects and necessary flow rates. For the Civic Center Plaza Fountain in downtown Albuquerque a scale model was built that was in itself the size of some complete fountains! With the mock-up the mechanical consultant examines possible distribution patterns, grouping various features with the same flow requirements together. With the total flow rate and the distribution pattern established, various options for pumping units to best serve the conditions and needs of the fountain are examined, and the most suitable pump is chosen in terms of the total dynamic head (tdh), total gallons per minute (gpm), available mechanical space clearances, and other factors.

The location of the equipment space will vary with every project, but it is obviously a good idea to keep it as inconspicuous as possible. For smaller fountains an underground vault adjacent to the fountain will suffice and will have a hatch cover for access. Larger water features will require a room that preferably has head clearance. The room is sometimes located in an adjacent building, although pipe runs usually make this option prohibitive. Access to mechanical rooms should be through a door, due to the frequency involved.

Since filter tanks and certain pumps must be entirely removed in cases of failure, access doors or hatches must be large enough to permit removal. A manual control valve should be provided on the suction side of the pump (as well as on the discharge side) to allow removal of the pump, if necessary, without draining the pool.

It is good practice to include basket strainers on the suction side of the pump and, with very small-orifice jets, in-line strainers on the discharge side to catch small particles that pass through the main suction screen. Since the velocity of water passing through the main suction screen affects the degree to which debris is attracted, it is very important to design the suction system to create a very low velocity. This is par-

tially accomplished by the size of the screens: the larger the screen area, the lower the velocity. These suction screens are often too small and will continually clog up.

Manual systems must be activated or shut off by maintenance personnel and also involve makeup water lines with manual valves and a manually operated drain. Automatic systems are usually used for larger and more complex systems in order to keep daily maintenance costs down. In these systems the pumps, makeup water systems, drains, display-feature valves, and filter system are all connected to a time clock or electrical control device. These systems allow for almost unlimited variations of display, with automatic time schedules programming the opening or closing of particular valves. These programmed installations sometimes involve pumping against closed valves and necessitate pumps equipped with seals that can withstand these pressure changes. Automatic systems range from very simple to sophisticated computer systems with intricate time cycles for changing effects, including lighting and sometimes music. These special-effect fountains are described in more detail later in this chapter.

PUMPS AND FILTER SYSTEMS

After all piping, valves, and nozzle requirements have been established, the pump can be properly sized for a fountain design. In all major fountain installations there are two completely independent systems of water recirculation. The *main recirculation system* draws water through a suction screen from a sump or from the body of the lowest pool, recirculates it through jets, and delivers it to higher-level basins and pools from which it has fallen, whether in the form of cascades, waterfalls, or basin overflow. The *filtering system* usually operates completely independently of this system and involves the turnover of much less water. Since the purposes are different, the suction points and discharge inlets are located with different criteria in mind. (In some older fountain installations part of the recirculating display water is run through a filter rather than using a separate pumping system, but this is no longer common.)

Pumps

Pumps have a rather interesting history, which I will not go into here, in terms of fountain design. The earliest ones involved manpower or horsepower and are recorded in old engravings and 18th-century books such as *Architecture Hydraulique* by Bernard Forrest Belidor. The earliest application of pumps to decorative water features took place in the 17th century: pumps were constructed by Louis XIV in 1682 at Marley to bring water to fountains at Versailles, but this particular operation never totally succeeded.

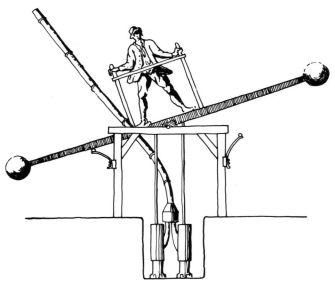

5-1. Two-cylinder manually operated pump depicted in 18th-century French book, *Architecture Hydraulique*, by Bernard Forrest Belidor.

The selection of a pump depends on a number of factors.

(1) *Required capacity.* This is rated in gallons per minute or gallons per hour.

(2) *Required pressure.* This is measured in feet of head or pounds per square inch. The total head is the sum of the suction lift, discharge elevation, friction loss, and head pressures required at the nozzles.

(3) *Source of supply.* This can be a pond, lake, collecting tank, or other source, any of which affects the suction conditions. Other factors are whether the supply is located above (suction head) or below (suction lift) the pump and how far away it is horizontally.

(4) *Type of power available.* This may be 110 or 220 volts, single-phase or three-phase, for example.

Most fountains require pumps to deliver a large volume of water at relatively low head pressures. Since very few fountains involve forcing water to a height more than 50' above the pump, high pressures are not called for. Pumps used for water displays are usually one of two general types.

(1) *Submersible pumps.* These are sometimes furnished along with jets and other equipment by fountain manufacturers as part of a kit and are placed directly on the bottom of the pool, preferably in a pit with a screen cover in a larger pool. These pumps are usually the best choice if less than 100 gallons per minute is to be pumped.

(2) *Dry or remote pumps.* These are located in a pit adjacent to the pool or in a mechanical-equipment room and are connected to the pool with piping.

It is sometimes feasible in larger fountain installations to use both remote dry pumps and submersible pumps to operate different parts of the system. A single jet or group of jets far removed from the main pump area may be more efficiently served by a separate submerged pump, while the dry pump operates the rest of the system.

Submersible fountain pumps, oil-filled with a 110-volt motor, are small pumps that usually range from $1/20$ to 1 horsepower and are most commonly used in small fountains in which relatively low volumes of water are involved. They involve no significant piping problems, require no equipment vaults, and are often used in conjunction with manual valves for both filling and draining the fountain. Small submersible pumps are capable of lifting approximately 120 gallons per hour to a height of 3' through a ½" pipe. Medium-sized submersible pumps are capable of delivering 10 to 15 gallons per minute through a ¾" to 1" discharge pipe, and the larger ⅓- to 1-horsepower pumps can deliver up to 100 gallons per minute through a 1¼" pipe.

Large-capacity submersible pumps are usually designed for pumping sewage and sometimes heavy industrial liquids and can range in size up to 50 horsepower and larger. These pumps do not merely sit on the bottom of the pool: they require a sunken pit, either in the pool or adjoining the pool, that is covered with a perforated brass sheet and an antivortex plate. Although these larger-size submersible pumps are typically more expensive than similar-sized dry pumps located outside the pool, the additional piping costs required to connect a remote pump often cancel the lower cost of the dry pump alone.

Dry centrifugal pumps are the most commonly used for large water features and range in size from ¼ to over 100 horsepower, with capacities up to 5,000 gallons per minute or greater. They are normally installed in pits or mechanical rooms adjacent to the intake-source pool, which is normally the lowest pool in a multilevel system. The suction side of the pump is located at an elevation below water level in the source pool and is connected to this pool by a suction line that slopes toward the pump. The suction line should terminate in an antivortex fitting or a depressed pit in the pool, since most pools are fairly shallow and can create a vortex condition over the suction end in shallow water. This condition, by drawing in air, greatly reduces the efficiency of the pump.

If currents caused by the suction line may be a problem—for example, in a long, narrow pool—it is best to locate the suction line in the center of the pool. A primary suction screen is placed over the suction pit to prevent debris from entering the pump and piping systems. A secondary, removable layer of polyethylene or fiberglass fly mesh may be placed over the fixed screen and held in place with galvanized pipes. This layer can then be picked up periodically and the debris dumped off. As debris gathers against a suction screen, the velocity of water entering the remainder of the screen increases and thus pulls debris toward the screen even faster. If the entire screen becomes blocked and no water is allowed to enter the suction line, the pumps will be damaged by running dry unless there is a safety control device that automatically shuts off the power to the pump if such a condition occurs.

All mechanical rooms or pits containing pumps must have both drainage and ventilation. As most pumps will leak some water as the seals wear, there should be drains and sump pumps in these areas if necessary. Ventilation is necessary to prevent condensation and to ensure the electric motors a proper life span; small ventilating fans are often also required.

A type of pump now commonly used in large water-feature installations is the *vertical mixed-flow pump.* It is usually used in city water systems at reservoir locations and in agricultural irrigation. These pumps are designed to sit in a concrete vault, with the base and suction fittings extending vertically below into a water-filled sump. They are used in conjunction with large fountains in or next to lakes and in water features that allow the mechanical vault to abut the source pool, in which case a pit inlet at the edge of the pool allows water to enter the water-filled sump under the pump without requiring a suction line to be placed directly into the pool itself. These pumps are more efficient than those requiring suction lines and avoid most vortex problems.

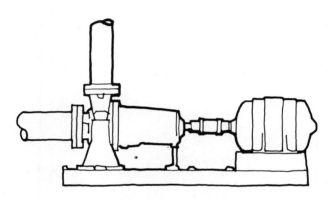

5-2. Centrifugal pump.

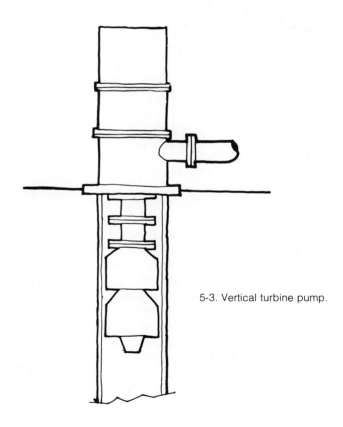

5-3. Vertical turbine pump.

Filter Systems

Filter systems for decorative fountain installations are essentially the same as swimming-pool filter systems and usually use equipment manufactured for that purpose. The equipment consists of the following.

(1) *Filter and pump.*

(2) *Skimmers.* These are installed at the waterline around the edge of the pool to draw off surface floating debris before it goes into suspension and sinks. Floating skimmers are sometimes used in the center of a pool to draw off material beyond the pull of the edge skimmers.

(3) *Suction device.* This is usually located in the deepest part of the pool to draw off lightweight debris on the bottom.

It should be kept in mind that large, shallow pools are very difficult to filter effectively, as they do not have the exaggerated bottom slope of swimming pools, which tends to force most debris to one end. More material that cannot be picked up by a filtering system, such as coins, is thrown into decorative pools than into swimming pools. There are two main types of filters used in conjunction with decorative fountains.

(1) *Diatomaceous-earth filter.* This has a layer of diatomaceous earth over a permeable surface inside a pressure tank. By means of a pressure gauge it can be determined when the filter layer has become sufficiently clogged to inhibit flow. At this time it is backwashed: that is, the flow through the filter is reversed, causing the earth layer with debris to be flushed out of the system into the drain line. These filters are able to trap smaller particles than can the sand filters. The disadvantage of this filter is that, each time that it is backwashed, a new layer of diatomaceous earth must be placed in the filter manually before reoperating.

(2) *Permanent-media sand filter.* In this filter water is pumped in through a medium usually composed of silica sand and back into the pool again. It must also be backwashed periodically but can be hooked up in an electrical control system to be done automatically, as there is no need to replace any filter material.

Swimming-pool filters are sized to provide a turnover of the total volume of pool water every 6 to 12 hours. Fountain filter systems, however, are generally sized in relation to the surface area of the pool rather than by total volume of water: swimming pools have a low ratio of water area to total volume compared to decorative pools. One rule of thumb used by some

designers is to provide 3 to 4 square feet of filter area for each 1,000 square feet of pool area. A high-rate sand filter will filter 15 to 20 gallons per minute per square foot of filter area.

Although somewhat dependent upon specific pool configuration and types of water features, one surface skimmer is usually provided for each 800 to 1,000 square feet of pool area. Some equipment people maintain that a skimmer should be located every 15' along the pool edge, which would increase the cost of the system considerably. One bottom suction—a standard floor drain—is probably sufficient for pool areas up to 2,000 square feet, but this also depends upon the detail design and the existence of trapped areas out of reach of surface skimmers. Although most pool skimmers are manufactured with an access lid or cover that is flush with the pavement around the pool, some designers find this hardware obtrusive and instead use skimmers with a front access.

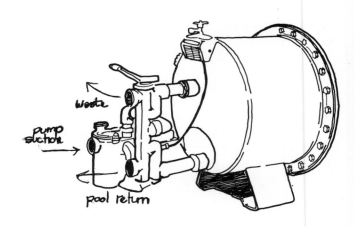

5-4. Typical permanent-media sand filter.

The return-discharge inlets of the filter system can often be designed to create currents in places that otherwise pose the problem of accumulating debris by locating discharge heads to direct the flow away from a certain area. These discharge heads are typically called *eyeball inlets,* as they are hemispheres that can be turned in a socket to direct the flow in various directions. They are usually mounted near the water surface and are directed downward and to the side. The rate of flow in these fittings is also adjustable, which allows the discharge in the system to be balanced by decreasing or increasing as required in an area. The location of skimmers and discharge inlets should also be influenced by prevailing winds, if any, which will cause debris to build up in certain areas.

As with swimming pools, there are always corners to be cleaned and debris that accumulates out of reach of the filter system. For this reason it is a good idea to include vacuum-inlet fittings, into which a vacuum-cleaner hose can be connected, as required at the edge of the pool. Some skimmers have vacuum-hose attachments included in the main housing. It is a good idea to include in the filter-system specifications a vacuum-cleaner hose, head, leaf rake, and pool brush, as these are all required as part of the general maintenance program.

OTHER COMPONENTS

Having dealt with the two major systems in any fountain design—the recirculating system and the filtration system—we can look at the smaller items that are somewhat incidental to the basic design but just as important for proper functioning of the total water system. Since a certain amount of water is always lost through evaporation, there must be a *water-level sensor* to measure the water level and automatically open a *water-makeup valve* to bring in fresh water up to the desired operating level. There must similarly be an *overflow drain* in case the water level becomes too high due to unusually intense rainfall or system malfunction. Each pool needs a *drain* at the lowest part of the bottom, with the bottom sloped to the drain. In a multilevel pool system, however, the lowest pool drawn through a filtering system usually has a bottom suction drain leading to the filter that can be used as the one and only drain. Charles Rapp, in a thesis entitled *Water in the Urban Landscape* (U.C. Berkeley, 1963), pointed out the importance of what he termed "hardware composition." As he explains, designers are often negligent in considering the overall effects of all the functional paraphernalia such as lighting, electrical-junction boxes, overflows, and inlets, thinking of these items as necessary evils rather than attempting to imaginatively weave them into the design. If this is the case, the hardware often becomes visually prominent and can detract considerably from the desired effect on the viewers. Items that stand on the pool bottom—such as certain light fixtures—or project above the water are of prime concern and should be thought of as an integral part of the overall design.

5-5. Overflow drains as a design element, Berger Fountain, Minneapolis.

Overflow Drains

All fountain catalogs illustrate overflow drains in the form of removable standpipes, with a little dome over the top to prevent leaves or other debris from blocking the opening. Although they are easy to install and can also serve as floor drains, many designers find them objectionable and use other means of handling the overflow, such as a side-wall overflow similar to a filtering-system skimmer; other details have also been used on sidewalls or under overhangs to act as overflow drains in as unobtrusive a manner as possible.

Water-level Sensors

Two main types of water-level sensors are used in fountain design. In smaller installations, in which the flow of makeup water is not great, a float control device consisting of a float-ball attached to a rod that acts as a level to open and close the fresh-water-supply valve is enclosed within a recessed niche box at the side of the pool, with a perforated cover to allow water into the box. These devices are strictly mechanical and do not require any electric switches or valves in order to function. The second type, which must be used in larger installations in which the flow of makeup water is too great to be handled by the float-ball device just described, is the electronic water-level sensor, which is also incorporated into the sidewall of the pool. These devices have two sensing rods that are cut or adjusted to the desired high- and low-water levels, with the difference in depth between the two rods representing the amount of water that is permitted to flow into the pool when the automatic makeup valve is energized by an electric signal. Conduits must be run from these sensors to control panels in the mechanical space, which are connected to the automatic valves.

Pool Chemicals

There are many pool chemicals on the market under proprietary trade names that are designed for a host of purposes, most for the swimming-pool industry. Some are designed to prevent algae; some are antifoam chemicals; some adjust alkalinity (the desirable range is pH 7.4 to 7.6); some are evaporation retardants. Most of the algicides, unlike chlorine, will not harm vegetation adjacent to the pool area. Some, such as Algimycin, are designed for small ornamental pools and will not even harm fish or aquatic plants. Full information on these chemicals is available through swimming-pool-equipment companies.

Heating

The operating season for water displays in colder climates may be extended considerably by including a water-heating system in the design. Larger fountain pools can utilize standard swimming-pool heaters. Heating the pool, however, is practical only if daytime temperatures are above freezing. When jets and cascades are operating, the effect of air cooling offsets the water heater. Objectionable steam may also rise from the surface of the pool. The operating season of some pools can be extended by adding antifreeze solutions such as ethylene glycol to the water, but this practice should be discouraged due to its potential harmful effects on vegetation and on humans or animals who happen to swallow some of the water. As mentioned in an earlier section, it is often both possible and desirable to allow ice mounds to build up during winter operation of fountains.

Special Controls

In addition to controlling the timing sequence of pump and jet operation electrically operated automatic controllers with time clocks can be used to change lighting effects. With dimmers on the lighting circuits lighting can be varied in harmony with changing water effects. Since both overall water effects and their effective lighting are more an art than a science, the installation of dimmers allows postinstallation adjustment for the optimum effect.

The simplest electric controller consists of an 110-volt clock motor that supplies power to a drive shaft with one or more cams, which vary the lighting and fountain effects through notches that activate small switches. Timing devices may be used for a wide variety of effects from raising and lowering the height of jets, alternating their operation, and varying lighting to programmed cycles so long that they do not give the impression of repeating themselves. The most sophisticated controllers are activated by music: specific notes are converted into electric impulses, thus activating automatic valves that create movement of water and changes of lighting in sequence with the music.

My personal feeling about most programmed fountains is that they deny the most delightful aspect of water, its uncontrolled, wild nature. These installations tend to merely show off modern gadgetry and technology, and they impress most people only superficially and momentarily. Practical economic considerations are also against them: the more complicated the electromechanical systems, the more the factors that can go haywire.

I have spent many enjoyable hours, however, as have thousands of others, sitting around the programmed International Fountain at Seattle Center on warm summer afternoons, listening to the music emanating from the hidden speakers of one of the world's largest stereophonic systems and watching the 217 jets continually rise and fall in sequence with the music, a spectacular and captivating display. If one accepts the desirability of combining highly sophisticated computer programming with fountain design, the possibilities for sequential display changes are almost infinite. All sorts of determinants could theoretically be programmed to affect the water display, from weather changes to people's voices. I feel, however, that these applications are often a sub-

5-6. Seattle Fountain. (Photo by Royal Cardon.)

stitute for imaginative design and cannot, even at their best, compensate for a poor concept.

A number of computer-programmed fountain installations have been built around the country, but by far the most sophisticated is the Horace E. Dodge & Son Memorial Fountain, designed by Noguchi for Detroit's civic-center plaza. The mechanical-electrical consultant on the project was Richard Chaix. The control system for this installation theoretically allows for a changing display that would not repeat itself during an 8-hour period. Its five pumps can deliver up to 17,000 gallons of water per minute to a series of nozzles that produce effects ranging from a solid column of water over 12' in diameter to upward-shooting jets, pulsating lights, and fog sprays. A special nozzle, developed for this project and patented by Noguchi, involves a double-wall cylinder 10″ in diameter with lights mounted in the center and water flowing between the two walls, which gives the effect of a solid column of water.

If a water display is located in an area in which wind may spray water out of a pool at certain times, the wind-control unit can be set to shut off the pumps and jets at a given wind speed before shutting them off completely if the wind reaches a higher level.

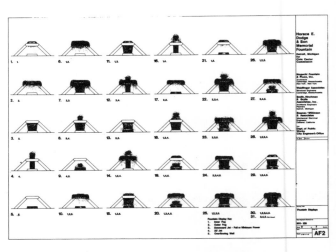

5-7. Programmed display chart for Horace E. Dodge & Son Memorial Fountain, Detroit, Noguchi Fountain & Plaza, Inc. (Photo by Noguchi Fountain & Plaza, Inc.)

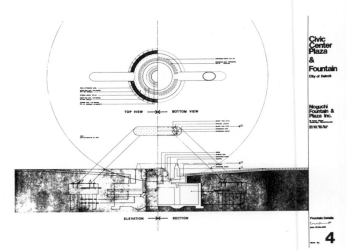

5-8. Dodge Fountain, Detroit, plan and section. (Photo by Noguchi Fountain & Plaza, Inc.)

5-9. Dodge Fountain, Detroit, assembly of the top ring. (Photo by John E. Green Co., Inc.)

5-10. Dodge Fountain, Detroit. (Photo by John E. Green Co., Inc.)

Lighting

Night lighting of water displays makes them an important and noticeable part of the evening landscape, sometimes transforming rather mundane fountains by day into quite attractive displays at night. I have seen a number of fountains that were completely unimpressive in the daytime but very striking under night illumination.

Water can be illuminated from within or from without, depending upon the specific circumstances. Floodlighting from outside the pool is much less expensive than underwater lighting. The primary consideration, and one that is often ignored, is to determine the overall ambient-lighting conditions provided by existing street lights and other adjacent lighting. This will influence the selection of lights and their placement within the design. Underwater lights are either mounted in the sidewalls, preferably shielded from direct eye contact, or installed flush with the bottom surface (either in a sunken pit or embedded in the concrete) or resting on heavy stands on the bottom. In order to ensure an even water temperature around the lenses to prevent breakage, underwater lights must be at least 2″ below the surface. Base-mounted lights are rather obtrusive during the daytime, are more prone to vandalism, and make it more difficult to sweep out debris when cleaning the pool. The objective, as with most lighting, is to let the viewer see the effects rather than the source of the lighting. One very effective way of lighting a pool is to install small, horizontally directed lights in the sidewalls just under the waterline, which will create a glowing body of water. Lights mounted under jets and waterfalls, illuminating them from below, are also very effective.

The most common lamps used in conjunction with underwater lighting fixtures are quartz lamps of various wattages, often 250 watts. These lamps are very small and permit the design of compact fixtures for which the lamp life span is quite long—these lamps are commonly used to light playing fields. Other lamps that have been used for their long life are 8,000-hour locomotive or traffic-signal incandescent lamps. Ground Fault Interrupters (GFIs) are now required by code whenever underwater light fixtures are used. These devices detect any leakage of current into the water or ground and immediately shut off the current before damage can be done. They are very sensitive to minute amounts of current leakage, so they must be

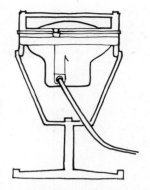

5-11. Base-mounted light fixture.

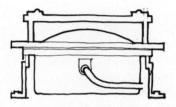

5-12. Flush-mounted light fixture with protective cover.

carefully adjusted to avoid nuisance tripping of the circuit breaker.

As fountain lights are one of the most common targets of vandalism, they must be equipped with rock guards of cast bronze with grills. Almost all fountain-light manufacturers provide these guards with their catalog lights, and they are a code requirement for all lights facing upward. Floodlighting from outside the pool is often desirable, particularly if the entire water feature is to be illuminated. Waterfalls and heavy jets may be lighted with spotlights that will reflect from the white water. By using the proper combination of lights moving patterns will be caused by reflections from streams of water as well as from the disturbed surface of the pool. While colored lights have often been used in water displays, often changing in programmed cycles, I feel that these effects are basically commercial and artificial and in no way comparable to the simpler use of clear or amber lights.

There are two methods of wiring fountain lights on the bottom of a pool: the first is to install an underwater junction box that can serve multiple lights; the second is to pass the light-fixture cord through a conduit on the bottom of the pool above water level. The latter method may prove impractical if there are a number of light fixtures that require separate conduits through the base of the pool. The junction box, on the other hand, if it is not embedded in the floor, is just one more piece of noticeable hardware. The best method to use is up to the discretion of the electrical-system designer, respecting the aesthetic considerations of the architect or landscape architect.

5-13. Effective night lighting of fountain, Case Western Reserve University, Cleveland, Ohio, William A. Behnke Associates. (Photo by William A. Behnke Associates.)

6. A GALLERY OF RECENT WATER FEATURES

In the midst of the hard surfaces, rigid forms, and mechanical sounds of the urban scene water presents itself as a fluid, ever-changing, tinkling or gushing element, a refreshing counterpoint to its surroundings if imaginatively used by the designer. Regardless of the particular type of design adopted for a water feature, the basic attraction that water has for city dwellers is its psychological link with nature: water has the ability to conjure up images of wild places even if it is used in a relatively controlled fashion. If this fact is always kept in mind and if the designer looks to the infinite expressions of water in nature, he will be better able to capture the essence of water to engage people's deepest reveries. In this final section I have assembled a sampling of various types of recent water features. Many of them are on a relatively monumental scale and involve high maintenance and operating costs, but they do offer excellent examples of good design by very capable firms fortunate enough to have had generous construction budgets to work with. There are a great many more examples of imaginative smaller fountains around the country that could fill another book; some of them are included in other parts of this text.

6-1, 6-2, 6-3, and 6-4. Peavey Plaza, Minneapolis, Minnesota, M. Paul Friedberg & Partners, landscape architects, Gerald Palevsky, mechanical consultant. (Photos by Shin Koyama.)

6-5 and 6-6. San Antonio Mall fountain, San Jose, California, Johnson, Leffingwell & Associates, landscape architects, Beamer/Wilkinson & Associates, mechanical consultants. (Photos by Jan Debye.)

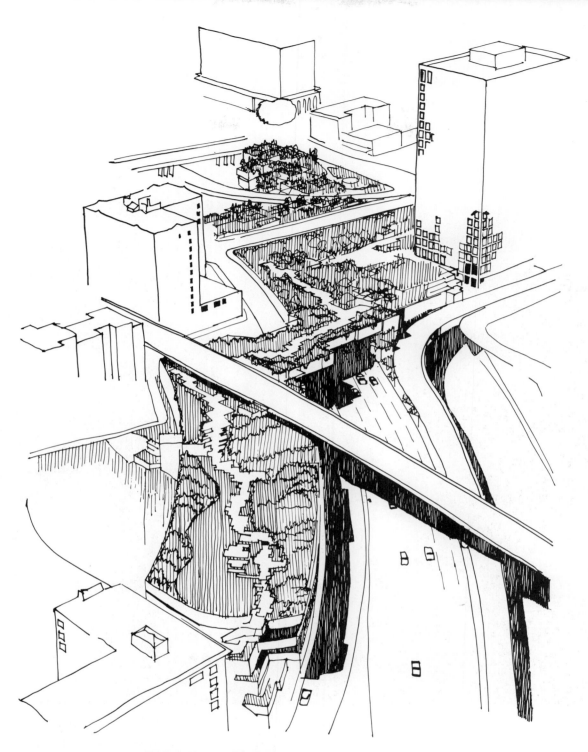

6-7 and 6-8. Seattle Freeway Park, Seattle, Washington. A unique 5.4-acre park, complete with cascades, a man-made canyon 32' high, and hanging gardens, bridges the freeway in downtown Seattle, providing an unexpected oasis. Three 125 h.p. pumps enclosed by a huge mechanical room under the park pump 10,000 gallons per minute of water over roaring cascades, drowning out the freeway traffic noise. Lawrence Halprin & Associates, landscape architects, Angela Danadjieva, project designer, Richard Chaix, fountain consultant. (Photo by Seattle Engineering Department.)

6-9 and 6-10 . State Street South Operations Center, Quincy, Massachusetts, M. Paul Friedberg and Partners, landscape architects. (Photos by Allen C. Pearson.)

6-11 and 6-12. Cedar West Fountain, Minneapolis, Minnesota, SWA Group, landscape architects. (Photos by SWA Group.)

6-13. First Plaza Fountain, Albuquerque, New Mexico, Harry
Weese & associates, architects.

6-14. Water stairs in Oakland City Center, SWA Group, landscape
architects (Photo by SWA Group.)

6-15. Ohlone College, Fremont, California. Decorative waterways using gravity flow in shallow runnels traverse the entire length of the hillside campus. SWA Group, landscape architects. (Photo by SWA Group.)

BIBLIOGRAPHY

Berrall, Julia S., *The Garden,* New York, The Viking Press, 1966

Byne, G., *Spanish Gardens and Patios,* Philadelphia, J.P. Lippincott Co., 1924

Cartocci, Sergio, *Tivoli and Its Artistic Treasure,* Rome, Oto Art Publishers, 1974

Engel, David, *Japanese Gardens for Today,* Rutland, Charles E. Tuttle Co., 1959

Erbe, Jack, *Handbook for Designing Fountains,* Albuquerque, Roman Fountains, Inc., 1974

Franck, Carl L., *The Villas of Frascati,* London, 1966

Gotthein, Marie Luise, *A History of Garden Art,* London, E.P. Dutton Co., 1928

Halprin, Lawrence, *Cities,* New York, Reinhold, 1963

Hubbard, Henry and Theodore Kimball, *Landscape Design,* New York, Macmillan, 1917

Jellicoe, Susan and Geoffrey, *The Use of Water in Landscape Architecture,* New York, St. Martin's Press, 1971

Joseph, James, *Poolside Living,* New York, 1963

Kirby, Rosina Greene, *Mexican Landscape Architecture,* Tuscon, University of Arizona Press, 1972

Latham, Charles, *The Gardens of Italy,* London, Country Life, 1905

Leopold, Luna and Langbein, Walter, *A Primer on Water,* U.S. Gov't. Printing Office

Leopold, Luna and Kenneth Davis, *Water,* New York, Time-Life Books, 1966

McCulley, Byron, *Water—Pools and Fountains,* ASLA Construction Handbook, McLean, Virginia, ASLA Foundation, 1976

Morton, H.V., *The Fountains of Rome,* New York, Macmillan, 1966

Muir, John, *The Yosemite,* 1912

Newton, Norman T., *Design on the Land,* Cambridge, Belknap Press, 1971

Nichols, R., *Spanish and Portuguese Gardens,* New York, Houghton Mifflin, 1924

Prieto-Moreno, Francisco, *Los Jardines de Granada,* Madrid

Rapp, Charles, *Water in the Urban Landscape,* M.A. thesis, U.C. Berkeley, 1963

Reynolds, John, *Windmills and Watermills,* New York, Praeger, 1970

Shepherd, John C. & Jellicoe, Geoffrey A., *Italian Gardens of the Renaissance,* London, Alec Tiranti Ltd., 1953

Siren, Osvald, *The Gardens of China,* New York, Ronald Press, 1949

Sordo, Enrique, *Moorish Spain,* New York, Crown Publishers, Inc., 1963

Switzer, Stephen, *An Introduction to a General System of Hydrostaticks and Hydraulicks, Philosophical and Practical,* London, 1729

Valentine, H.R., *Water in the Service of Man,* Baltimore & London, Penguin, 1967

Villa-Real, Ricardo, *The Alhambra and the Generalife,* Madrid, 1974

Villiers-Stuart, C.M., *Spanish Gardens,* London, B.T. Batsford, Ltd., 1929

Villiers-Stuart, C.M., *Gardens of the Great Mughals,* London, A. and C. Black, 1913

Wilbur, Donald, *Persian Gardens and Garden Pavillions,* Rutland, Charles E. Tuttle, 1962

Wolfflin, Heinrich, *Renaissance and Baroque,* Ithaca, 1966

INDEX